WORSHIPERS OF TI

Call (516) 8

1. More Books
2. Anointed Throne Room Worship CDs
3. Instructional DVD on how to worship in the Throne Room of the Living God
4. Prayer shawls, shofars, and anointing oil from Israel
5. The Tenach book - the original Hebrew translation of the Old Testament (the original meaning will astound you)
6. To make arrangement for worship gatherings at your church
7. For prayer

CREDENTIALS

Evangelist Jacob Toback has preached in the streets of New York for almost 20 years by the grace of God. He has done evangelistic outreach in the Caribbean islands of Jamaica. The Lord has used him to help build the Teen Challenge Drug Center in Long Island, New York.

The mandate we have received from the Lord for this ministry is to reestablish true priestly throne room worship according to the Word of God and not according to deadritualistic tradition of man.

ORDINATION

Evangelist Jacob Toback was formally and publicly ordained by the renowned Lions Roar Ministry International, P.O. Box 751, Oakland, Florida 34760. Bishop David Braland, president and founder.

The mandate we have received for this ministry is to reestablish true priestly worship of the Holy of Holies in the body of Christ instead of traditionalistic ritualism.

If you are led to help us to get this message to the body of Christ, please send your gifts to continue printing this book to:

JACOB TOBACK
Worshipers of the Living God Ministries
P.O. BOX 881895
PORT SAINT LUCIE, FL 34988-1895

Anointed Holy of Holies worship CDs
available for a gift of $ 10 per CD.

NO FLESH STANDS IN THE HOLY OF HOLIES

NO FLESH STANDS IN THE HOLY OF HOLIES

The hidden key
to true priestly
THRONE ROOM WORSHIP.

NEW YORK CITY EVANGELIST
JACK TOBACK

Mall Publishing, Co.

THE PRINTED WORD THE PLANTED SEED

NILES, ILLINOIS

Published by:
Mall Publishing Company
5731 West Howard Street
Niles, Illinois 60714
877.203.2453

All scriptures, quotations are from the Amplified Version of the Bible.
All original Hebrew quotations are from the The Tanach Stone Edition.
Actual pages taken from The Tanach Stone Edition, published by Mesorah
Publication, LTD; Psalms 29, page 1459 and Psalms 96, page 1521.

Book Designed by April Cass of AprilCass Design
Book Cover Illustration by George Popichak of gp illustration/design

ISBN 0-9741022-6-1

For licensing / copyright information, for additional copies
or for use in specialized settings contact:

Jacob Toback

Worshipers of the Living God Ministries

P.O. Box 881895
Port Saint Lucie, FL 34988-1895
(516) 840-0800 or (516) 330-0995

Printed in the United States of America

—·—·—·—·—·—·—·—

This book is dedicated to
the dearly beloved whole Body of Christ who include
my wife Nancy, my children, Douglas, Greg, Shannon, Todd,
and Daniel. Also, my step children, Tommy and Tracy,
my daughters-in-law Diana, Janine, and Julie,
my son-in-law John, all of my grandchildren, which God has
blessed me with, Gabbie, Jaqueline, Austin, Ashley, Ethan,
Hannah, John Jr., Logan, plus, Mom and Dad.

—·—·—·—·—·—·—·—

Freely I receive and freely I give you a key. The Lord has already told me some will try to dispute this book. However, as hard as they try, they will not be able to. The reason they will not be able to is because the words in this book are from above, not below. Everything said in this book is backed up by THE LIVING WORD OF GOD. His word - not a man's. As you read each page carefully take a pencil and underline anything that you think is not of God or his will. I invite you in all earnestness to call me at our ministry number.

However, if you do see this as the truth, the Lord expects a response from you in your actions at home and in church. Those who embrace these truths will be able to draw closer to him than ever before. Those who refuse to respond will see him only at a distance!

CONTENTS

INTRODUCTION

The church buildings are getting bigger and more beautiful. The sound equipment is becoming more sophisticated. The music is getting louder, longer, and more creative. It can even be played while a message is being preached to get people in the "mood". More books are being written than ever before. More people are claiming to know God than ever before. There are more worship groups traveling around the country "entertaining church goers" than ever before and some are very anointed. There are more people taking titles of apostles, bishops, evangelists, and pastors than ever before. During our worship service we can hear our people crying out "Jesus is Lord of All." "Our God is Holy." "There is none like Him." "He is creator of heaven and earth" and "There is no other God like our God." At the same time our worship leaders are singing the words, "Take me in to the Holy of Holies." "I've come to worship you only." "We bow down before you, we kneel down before you." "We bring honor to your Holy Name."

This is what our people sing. However, what we sing and what we are doing are two completely different things.

With all these activities, functions, and words we sing all we have to do is look at one single thing to see the "fruits" of all this. You will now see there is something terribly wrong. Just observe for yourself during "intense worship" at a typical Sunday service at most any church you could walk into, just how many people are on their knees, bowed, or prostrated before the Holy One of Israel. In a church of one thousand, you could not count them on ten fingers.

1

This says it all! Nothing more has to be said on this subject. Our God, who is our Father, His Son, and the Holy Spirit, have not yet to be honored properly before our assembly or the world! The worship in our churches today does not match to the heavenly pattern of worship.

By those who come near me I will be treated as Holy. And before all the people, I will be honored. Leviticus 10:3

See for yourself, for the first time ever the (Ancient "key" from the original Hebrew translation that has been fenced in and hidden from our eyes but has now been revealed by the Holy Spirit. This key word שָׁחָה shâchâh revealed directly from the Hebrew scripture will bring the weight of the glory of God down not only personally but also corporately in our worship services.

Many books have been written about worship but absolutely *NONE have had this "ancient key" from the original Hebrew scripture included in their writings.* This **KEY** holds the secret to RELEASING God's presence like a flowing river in our church. IT IS NOT THAT God's PRESENCE ISN'T ALREADY HERE. IT IS! The problem is we are not approaching him acceptably. WE MUST APPROACH HIM HEAVEN'S WAY, NOT OURS! For those who read this and ACT on the truths contained in this book, which line up exactly with the Word of God, your lives will be transformed immediately and forever!

1

OUR WORSHIP IS NOT GIVING HONOR TO GOD

Many of our churches have been crying out for the Lord to let the weight of his glory fall, or maybe a better term, his tangible presence to be experienced. We seem to be waiting for him to do something, when all this time he is waiting now for us to do something. The Lord at this time is saying, "I have heard your prayers, I will not frustrate you. I am your loving Father. I have given you the EXCLUSIVE rights to enter the Holy of Holies, where nobody can enter but those who have been washed by the blood of the Lamb of God. By those who have a heart that truly desires *intimacy* with me, not just in words, but action that back up those words. *By those who spend much time with me in the secret place.* My word says when you seek me with all your heart, you will find me."

Then you will seek Me, inquire for, and require Me [as a vital necessity] and find Me when you search for Me with all your heart.
Jeremiah 29:13

3

"My word cannot lie," says the Lord.

What is the Lord waiting for? He is waiting for us to approach him in worship the only proper, priestly way. He is waiting for us to approach him like Abraham, Moses, Daniel, David, Apostle Paul, Peter, All of Heaven, and the way the word of God tells us to. What is the correct way? *The pattern of the worship must match heavenly worship.* The Holy One of Israel has always had a pattern for his priests. The fact of the matter is we are his priests.

And formed us into a kingdom (a royal race), priests to His God and Father – to Him be the glory and the power and the majesty and the dominion throughout the ages and forever and ever. Amen. Revelation 1:6

And now they sing a new song, saying, You are worthy to take the scroll and to break the seals that are on it, for You were slain (sacrificed), and with Your blood You purchased men unto God from every tribe and language and people and nation. And you have caused them to become God's kingdom and his priests and they will reign on the earth. Revelation 5:9

In Exodus, God commanded Moses, and Moses taught Aaron and his sons, and the other priests how to minister before the Lord. The problem is not only do the priests of the Body of Christ not know how to minister before the Lord, but even worse, *Pastors and worship leaders are completely in the dark.* Why? Because Satan has stolen the worship from the church, without them even being aware of it. We have literally been lulled to sleep. Our most precious intimacy of worship has been deliberately misplaced by the enemy, and in its place we have *a dead ritualistic form of worship* with most of the Body of Christ. Except for the very, very few that are hearing the uttering of the soft and gentle voice of the Holy Spirit, which is saying "Match the pattern of worship to the pattern of Heavenly worship."

You will seek me and you will find me, if you search for me with all your heart. Jeremiah 29:13

2

THE CALL
TO THE MOUNTAIN

Please read the following pages very carefully. What you are about to read will surely change the relationship forever that you have with our Heavenly Father, His Beautiful Son, and the Holy Spirit. No matter how close you think you are with him, you are going to experience him in a way you never thought possible. If you are a pastor or a worship leader, *you are going to receive a key delivered by the Holy Spirit himself into your hands that will allow the tangible presence, the weighty glory of God to fall in your particular church.* How do I know? Because what I'm giving you did not come from me. It came from the Holy One in the secret place. He showed me, I wrote it down and practiced it. It's true and you will know it's true because it's backed up by the very word of God. In nineteen years of services, I have never heard this preached. I have been a street preacher for eighteen years in Manhattan. I use sound amplification equipment to do worship and preaching to the lost. I am Jewish and the Lord revealed himself to me in a Zen Buddha temple, appearing to me on the cross. He said, "You are to worship no other God but me," and since that experience, that is exactly what I've done.

5

I was preaching in Manhattan on 32nd and Broadway, exactly the time that the Twin Towers fell. I preached most of that day and I have never experienced anything like that in my life. People were holding hands in the street, twenty-five people at one time praying in the streets of Manhattan. People were desperate. They were looking for an answer. Many hearts opened to Christ that day.

When I returned home in the late afternoon, little did I know the fingerprints of the Lord would be on the door handle of my house. A voice simply said to me, "I want you to pray in the garage from now on." Our garage is located in a detached building in the back of my house. It is private with no phone or disturbances in it. The Lord was going to take me on a journey that would cause me to see his face as never before. To have me climb towards the top of the mountain and understand *what the priesthood and intimacy in worship really means. He would give me the keys to unlock the secret of what acceptable, priestly worship is and the blueprint for every church on the face of the earth of the way to come into his true presence.*

This book is not about war stories in the ministry. It's not about what God did yesterday or what he intends to do tomorrow. It's not about chasing God all over the country to find his presence at a particular place.

It is about God truly pouring himself out upon you NOW – not tomorrow. It is about receiving the true experience of his tangible presence and power. He is a *today God* for his children. In this book, the Holy Spirit promises you the *real and authentic key that will open heaven for you in worship immediately.*

It is not a new key, but an old one. It is from the *original Hebrew scriptures* and for whatever reason has been mostly eliminated from our King James Version. You have never read this or been preached to about this ancient key before.

Once I separated myself in the garage, within two weeks, I heard his voice say, "Come up to the mountain." I knew it meant to deliberately seek his face. I immediately increased my prayer time to 3 hours per day and was fasting twice a week. I made sure I wrote in my journal what he would say to me each and every day. He made

me aware of the priesthood that each and every one of his children
have been called to. I always read about it in scripture,

*And formed us into a kingdom (a royal race), priests to His God
and Father – to Him be the glory and the power and the majesty
and the dominion throughout the ages and forever and ever. Amen.*
Revelation 1:6

*but never had the revelation of it being a particular position or
function until now.* The Lord told me this. These are his exact
words and they apply to each and every one of us.

*WORSHIP IS THE HIGHEST CALLING THAT EXISTS IN MY
KINGDOM.* TO WORSHIP AT MY FEET IN THE HOLY OF
HOLIES. I HAVE GIVEN THOSE WHO ARE CALLED BY MY
NAME THIS HOLY ACCESS, YET VERY FEW TAKE ADVAN-
TAGE. THEY WILL DO EVERYTHING AND ANYTHING
ELSE, BUT THE *ONE THING* I REQUIRE OF MY TRUE SER-
VANTS. THAT IS TO *WORSHIP* AND TO *PRAY.* AND TO *PAY
HOMAGE* TO THEIR FATHER AND MY SON. THIS IS WHAT
I'M CALLING YOU TO DO FOR ME. I'M CALLING YOU TO
MY FEET. I'M CALLING YOU INTO THE HOLY OF HOLIES.
INTO THE HOLIEST PART OF HEAVEN, WHERE THE
SERAPHIMS AND CHERUBIMS SING. WHERE THE TWEN-
TY-FOUR ELDERS BOW AT THE CRY OF HOLY, HOLY,
HOLY. I'M CALLING YOU FOR THE SERVICE TO WORSHIP
ME. DO NOT LOOK AROUND YOU AT MAN. DO NOT TRY
TO CONFORM TO MAN'S WAY OF SERVICE OR WHAT HE
THINKS I WANT. YOU MUST PAY ATTENTION TO WHAT I
WANT YOU TO DO FOR ME. WHAT I REQUIRE. WHAT I AM
PLEASED WITH. LISTEN TO THE SOFT STILL VOICE OF
THE SPIRIT OF THE HOLY ONE AND I WILL LEAD YOU
INTO THE HIDDEN MYSTERIES OF MY KINGDOM, I WILL
THEN BE ABLE TO FLOW THROUGH YOU AS I WISH. YOU
MUST OBEY THE CALL. SIT AT MY FEET TO WORSHIP, TO
GAZE, TO MEDITATE, TO COMMUNE. *COME OUT FROM
THE WORLD, TOUCH NOT THE AMBITIONS OF MAN, BUT
TOUCH THE DESIRES OF MY HEART!*

The Lord then quickened me to *John 4:23. (Amplified)*

A time will come, however, indeed it is already here, when the true (genuine) worshippers will **worship** *the Father in* **spirit** *and in* **truth (reality)***; for the Father is* **seeking** *just such people as these as His worshippers.*

God is a spirit (a spiritual being) and those who worship Him must worship Him in spirit and in truth (reality). Study this scripture. **Note: We must not only worship Him, but also worship Him in spirit and truth.** *To know* that he is *right* here with us every time we *pray*, and every time we *sing.* He hears *every* word, and *every* song. *This is the truth.* Since he is a spirit, we must approach him the way the spiritual world approaches him.

What stood out for me was when we pray we seek him. *When we worship in spirit and in truth he seeks us.* Imagine God is seeking out those who are willing to worship as priests of the most high God. This caused me to have a fierce desire to become a worshipper that he wanted to seek after.

My prayer became, *"Lord, take me higher into praise and worship, and deeper into prayer intercession. Teach me how to fulfill the ministry of the priesthood."* This prayer became my passion.

Before this happened I always had a great prayer and worship life that consisted of a couple hours a day. But now, for the first time, I realized my Heavenly Father, who is the God of Abraham, Isaac, and Jacob, and his dear son Jesus Christ with the Holy Spirit, truly wanted me to come into their presence. They wanted me to seek their face in prayer and worship and to sit at their feet *and just worship before anything else.* They truly wanted to have a close intimacy with me. They were truly real. They could hear each word I prayed and each song I sung to them. Sometimes it's so hard to believe it's real – but it truly is. The Lord told me how "jealous" he was for his children. How he desires more than anything else to just fellowship with us. He desires so much that we love him more than anything else.

Throughout my Christian life I always wanted to know his love for me, but now I realize He also wants us to love him passionate-

ly. I understand now the commandment – Love the Lord your God with all your heart, soul, strength, and mind. The Lord told me he wanted me to love him more than life itself. This brought me to another prayer. *"Enlarge my heart to love you more than life itself."*
By becoming aware of him – I was becoming aware of his presence. This was becoming *my priority in my life*. Now that I knew how much he was seeking me as a worshipper, it caused me to put my worship and prayer time before my business, preaching, and anything else in my life. I tried to cut out everything that took time away from seeking him, except for, of course, my family.

I realized the reason for living another day *was to worship our great God, the Father, the Son and the Holy Spirit.* This is the reason we live.

*And now they sing a new song, saying, You are worthy to take the scroll and to break the seals that are on it, for You were slain (sacrificed), and with Your blood You purchased men unto God from every tribe and language and people and nation. **Verse 10:** And You have made them a kingdom (royal race) and priests to our God, and they shall reign [as kings] over the earth!* Revelation 5:9,10

I was actually reaching into the throne room, having dialogue and an intimacy with my Father, his Son Lord Jesus as never before.

Then the Lord answered me on a prayer that I could have never imagined possible. I prayed from the scripture from Jeremiah 33:3.

Call to Me and I will answer you and show you great and mighty things, fenced in and hidden, which you do not know (do not distinguish and recognize, have knowledge of and understand) Jeremiah 33:3.

He brought me into the reality of the throne room and how Heavenly worship is conducted!

9

3

OUR WORSHIP MUST MATCH THE HEAVENLY PATTERN OF WORSHIP

Please pay close attention! You have never heard this preached, and again it will be backed up by the word of God. It will be a *key* that will open up to you the reality of his presence.

As kings and priests, we are able to supernaturally enter into the Holy of Holies directly at his feet where the mercy seat is. The blood of Jesus is sprinkled on the mercy seat. He is the perfect sacrifice. That's where our confidence lies.

Therefore, brethren, since we have full freedom and confidence to enter into the [Holy of] Holies [by the power and virtue] in the blood of Jesus.

By this fresh (new) and living way which He initiated and dedicated and opened for us through the separating curtain (veil of the Holy of Holies), that is, through His flesh, And since we have [such] a great and wonderful and noble Priest [Who rules] over the house of God, Let us all come forward and draw near with true

11

(honest and sincere) hearts in unqualified assurance and absolute conviction engendered by faith (by that leaning of the entire human personality on God in absolute trust and confidence in His power, wisdom, and goodness), having our hearts sprinkled and purified from a guilty (evil) conscience and our bodies cleansed with pure water. So let us seize and hold fast and retain without wavering the hope we cherish and confess and our acknowledgement of it, for He Who promised is reliable (sure) and faithful to his word.
Hebrews 10:19-23 (Amplified)

Now that you understand why you have the confidence to actually be in the throne room, which is where you'll worship and pray, what do you see? What does the worship look like? *Remember our worship must match the heavenly worship.* This has been God's design from the very beginning of time.

Our father who is in heaven, hallowed be your name, your kingdom come, your will be done (held holy and revered) on earth as it is in heaven. Luke 11:2 (Amplified)

That's right, your will be done in our worship in our *prayer closets* and *church worship services* as it is in heaven.

Now understand this, when we are in our prayer closets or church services we should have entered into the holy of Holies, which is in heaven, even though we are on the earth. Don't try to understand it. Just except what God's word says. It is a spiritually, supernatural happening. But nevertheless, it is reality.

So then, let's understand, if we are coming into God's kingdom (which is our kingdom also, because Christ lives in us) we must approach the Holy of Holies as one who lives in the heavenly kingdom or we are out of place. We can not enter into worship in the throne room by the church's way or our own way. It must be God's way. Again, we are a Heavenly being. We have been given joint seating with Christ himself.

And he raised us up together with him and made us sit down together (giving us joint seating with him) in the heavenly sphere (by virtue of our being) in Christ Jesus (the Messiah, the Anointed One). Ephesians 2:6

In other words, supernaturally we live in the heavenlies but we serve on the earth. As priests this is how we function.

Most of us are living our lives on this earth. We are tied to it. Our devotion is to it. We have no idea that we are crucified with Christ. It is no longer I who live, but Christ who lives inside me. As Jesus said, "This *kingdom is not mine. My kingdom is from above – this kingdom is from below.*" And now we also say our kingdom is from above, not below.

Now you are going to understand the pattern of heavenly worship and the key that was stolen from us. It will be given back to those who are willing to take it. *He who has ears listen to what the Spirit is saying to you now.*

Read Revelations chapters 4 and 5 over and over and over, until the Spirit engraves the throne room in your heart. In chapter 4, John the apostle is taken up to the throne room of God. At the beginning of Revelations he is told to write this down. Why? So that you and I right now can understand what has been fenced in and hidden until now.

We see the Holy One. Now we will see exactly what the throne room looks like in detail. This is the Holy of Holies, where we enter in to worship God. We as priests who have been washed in the blood of the lamb have exclusive access. *Pay attention very carefully. Why? Because the Holy Spirit will start to teach us as priests how to approach the Lord in his throne room.*

After this I looked, and behold, a door standing open in the heaven! And the first voice which I had heard addressing me like [the calling of] a war trumpet said, Come up here, and I will show you what must take place in the future.

At once I came under the [Holy] Spirit's power, and behold, a throne stood in heaven, with One seated on the throne! And He Who sat there appeared like [the crystalline brightness of] jasper and [the fiery] sardius, and encircling the throne there was a halo that looked like [a rainbow of emerald. Twenty-four other thrones surrounded the throne, and seated on these thrones were twenty-four elders (the members of the Heavenly Sanhedrin), arrayed in white clothing, with crowns of gold upon their heads. Out from the throne came flashes of lightning and rumblings and peals of thunder, and in front of the throne seven blazing torches burned, which are the seven Spirits of God [the sevenfold Holy Spirit]; And in front of the throne there was also what looked like a transparent glassy sea, as if of crystal. And around the throne, in the center at each side of the throne, were four living creatures (beings) who were full of eyes in front and behind [with intelligence as to what is before and at the rear of them].

The first living creature (being) was like a lion, and the second living creature like an ox, the third living creature had the face of a man, and the fourth living creature [was] like a flying eagle.

And the four living creatures, individually having six wings, were full of eyes all over within [underneath their wings]; and day and night they never stop saying, Holy, holy, holy is the Lord God Almighty (Omnipotent), Who was and Who is and Who is to come. And whenever the living creatures offer glory and honor and thanksgiving to Him Who sits on the throne, Who lives forever and ever (through the eternities of the eternities).

The twenty-four elders (the members of the heavenly Sanhedrin) fall prostrate before Him Who is sitting on the throne, and they worship Him Who lives forever and ever; and they throw down their crowns before the throne, crying out, Worthy are You, our Lord and God, to receive the glory and the honor and the dominion, for You created all things; by Your will they were [brought into being] and were created. Revelation 4: 1-10

We see God being worshiped first by the four living creatures. They cry out day and night Holy, Holy, Holy! This is then followed by the twenty-four elders casting their golden crowns before the throne and prostrating themselves and saying worthy is he to receive glory and honor. Notice that they are not standing but laying down before the throne which is called prostrating.

Remember I said before, as Jesus said, my kingdom is from above, this kingdom is from below (earth). Since Jesus lives in us and we have joint seating with him at the throne spiritually speaking our worship *must match the pattern of heaven not earthly worship of men who have their own ideas or formulations but have nothing to do with the Kingdom of God.*

In short, *no flesh stands or sits in the throne room.* No spiritual beings will stand in the throne room! Why? Because He is the Holy One of Israel. The God of Abraham, Isaac, and Jacob. The creator of Heaven and Earth. Jesus, on the other hand, has been exalted from the lowest part of the earth, to the highest part of heaven and sits at the right hand of the Father. He is called the Alpha and Omega, who was, who is, and is to come – The Lord God.

Saying, I am the Alpha and the Omega, the First and the Last. Write promptly what you see (your vision) in a book and send it to the seven churches which are in Asia - to Ephesus and to Smyrna and to Pergamum and to Thyatira and to Sardis and to Philadelphia and to Laodicea. Then I turned to see [whose was] the voice that was speaking to me, and on turning I saw seven golden lampstands, And in the midst of the lampstands [One] like a Son of Man, clothed with a robe which reached to his feet and with a girdle of gold about His breast. His head and His hair were white like white wool, [as white] as snow, and His eyes [flashed] like a flame of fire. His feet glowed like burnished (bright) bronze as it refined in a furnace, and His voice was like the sound of many waters. In his right hand He held seven stars, and from His mouth there came forth a sharp two-edged sword, and His face was like the sun shining in full power at midday. When I saw Him, I fell at His feet as if dead. But he laid His right hand on me and said, Do not be afraid! I am the First and the Last, And the Ever-living One [I am living in the eternity of the eternities]. I died, but see I am alive forevermore; and I possess the keys of death and Hades (the realm of the dead). Write therefore the things you see, what they are [and signify] and what is to take place hereafter. As to the hidden meanings (the mystery) of the seven stars you saw on My right hand and the seven lampstands of gold: the seven stars are the seven angels (messengers) of the seven assemblies (churches) and the seven lampstands are the seven churches. Revelation 1:11-20

I repeat - Nobody stands before the Holy One in the throne room of the Living God. They kneel, they bow, or they prostrate, but THEY DO NOT STAND OR SIT! It is illegal and unacceptable in heaven and therefore illegal and unacceptable on earth.

Truly I tell you, whatever you forbid and declare to be improper and unlawful on earth must be what is already forbidden in heaven, and whatever you permit and declare proper and lawful on earth must be what is already permitted in heaven. Matthew 18:18

Let me say this. There is a time when we get intimate with our Heavenly Father and crawl up into his lap. There is a time that Jesus is our best friend who we can laugh with. But we also must know that when we enter the Holy of Holies to worship, our Father is the Lord God Almighty and Jesus is the righteous judge. *They must be reverenced acceptably.*

The reverent and worshipful fear of the Lord is the beginning and the principal and choice part of knowledge [its starting point and its essence]; but fools despise skillful and godly Wisdom, instruction, and discipline. Proverbs 1:7

Webster dictionary defines:

Reverence: 1) A feeling of deep respect, mixed with wonder, fear, and love 2) A deep bow 3) The condition of being greatly respected and venerated.

Worship: To pay great honor and respect; Revere venerate; To consider extremely precious; Hold very deep; Adore

Render unto Hashem honor worthy of his name: take an offering,
and come to his courtyards. Prostrate yourselves before Hashem in
his intensely holy place; tremble before Him, everyone on earth.
Declare among the nations, "Hashem has reigned."
Psalms 96:8-10 (original Hebrew translation)

4

THE ANCIENT KEY TO
TRUE PRIESTLY WORSHIP

Now let's talk about the church and ourselves, and then I'm going
to give you the key that the Holy Spirit Himself showed me. It is
something that you've never heard preached, but is going to change
your worship, the church's worship, and is going to usher in the
glory of God.

Let's look at the church worship. During worship most people
stand, some sit, and very few kneel, bow or prostate themselves. To
clarify, during praise it is acceptable to stand. Praise is when we
give honor and thanks to God for what He has done. We are then in
the outer courts.

However, when the worship leader takes us to worship, we are
stepping in the Holy of Holies. *We are now giving God honor for*
who He is.

When Moses who was instructed by God to teach the priesthood
to Aaron and his sons only one priest from the whole nation could

enter into this most Holy place. He had to be cleansed by the blood of sacrificial animals. This was the High Priest.

You and I, after cleansing ourselves, have the access into the Holy of Holies by the blood of the Lamb Jesus Christ.

Never standing, but always kneeling, bowing, or prostrating ourselves.

Our churches today, from the biggest to the smallest have absolutely no concept of the acceptable way to approach God as priests and kings. We have giant size churches with sophisticated sound equipment and everything organized to the inch, but we're missing the most important thing – *the knowledge of the priesthood!*

Some churches have been crying out to God for His glory to fall. He hears and wants to come, *but we must receive him in the acceptable manner according to the Word of God.* We know that the Lord has a pattern for everything.

David the King and a great man of God wanted the presence of God more than anyone. He was a man after God's own heart and loved the Lord dearly. He attempted to bring the Ark of the Covenant back to Jerusalem. He mounted the Ark on an oxen cart and wound up having the Lord strike dead a soldier who attempted to touch the ark as it was falling off the cart. It was good intentions, but a wrong approach to the Holy things of God.

David greatly feared the Lord that day but later learned the proper manner of how to handle the Ark and the presence of God. The Ark had to be put on the shoulders of the priests rather than a beast. Then the glory fell.

David had to learn from mistakes. *We also have to learn when revelation is given from the Holy Spirit.* The question is this, when the Holy Spirit speaks to you and of course it must be backed up by scripture, are you willing to humble yourself before the Lord and submit to his way? Are you willing to do what's right in the sight of the Lord, even if it means possibly persecution from the Body of Christ itself? Are you willing to please the Father, the Son, and the Holy Spirit and gain his tangible presence in your life and in the church even if it means some or many may forsake you? If you are, I will now give you the keys to the truth of what we have been talking about.

You will be shocked at what you are going to see, and without a doubt, understand why our church worship in most cases is man's dead ritualistic formalism.

He who has ears, listen to what the Spirit is saying. The Tenach is the Hebrew old testament. It starts with Genesis and goes to Malachi. It's written in Hebrew on one side and translated to English on the opposite column. You may purchase it in any store that sells Jewish books or even Christian bookstores. *The Old Testament from Genesis to the prophet Malachi was originally written in Hebrew.*

Now listen carefully. Shockingly, when you look at the Tenach, most every time you come to the place where the word worship was used in the King James Version, the original Hebrew translates in the Tenach to bow down, kneel, and prostrate.

In other words, the King James Bible we have been reading says worship, however the true original Hebrew scripture is saying *bow down, kneel, and prostrate.* The Hebrew word for worship is שָׁחָה shâchâh. It means to humble, prostrate in homage to royalty or God. Bow (self) down, crouch, fall down (flat), humbly beseech, do or make obeisance, kneel, reverence, make to stoop, worship. (can be found in Strong's Concordance – Hebrew & Chaldee dictionary page 114, word 7812)

When the Holy Spirit showed me this, I was totally awed at what I was seeing. How in the world had this escaped our Bibles? How in the world has this been actually stolen from the Body of Christ?

Let Me Show You Examples:
(King James Version)

1. Ascribe to the Lord, O mighty ones
   Ascribe to the Lord, glory and strength
2. Ascribe to the Lord, the glory due to his name
   Worship the Lord in the splendor of his holiness
   Psalms 29:1-2

19

Original Hebrew translation from Tenach
1. Render unto (Hashem honor and might
2. Render unto Hashem the honor due his name, bow to Hashem in the beauty of holiness.
Psalms 29:1-2

*Please note: the King James uses the word worship, the original Hebrew translates to bow

(King James Version)

6. Honor and majesty are before him
Strength and beauty are in his sanctuary
7. Give unto the Lord, O ye kindred's of the people
Give unto the Lord glory and strength
8. Give unto the Lord the glory due unto his name
Bring an offering, and come into his courts
9. O worship the Lord in the beauty of his holiness
Fear before him, all the Earth Psalms 96:6-9 (KJV)

Original Hebrew translation from the Tenach
6. Glory and majesty are before him, might and splendor in his sanctuary
7. Render unto Hashem, O families of the peoples, render unto Hashem honor and might
8. *Render unto Hashem honor worthy of his name; take an offering and come to his courtyards.*
9. *Prostrate yourselves before Hashem in his intensely holy place tremble before Him, everyone on Earth.* Psalms 96:6-9

Please note again that the King James Version uses the word worship, and the original Hebrew uses the word prostrate.

7812. שָׁחָה shâchâh, shaw-khaw'; a prim, root; to depress, ie. prostrate (espec. reflex in homage to royalty or God):–bow (self) down, crouch, fall down (flat), humbly beseech, do (make) obeisance, do reverence, make to stoop, worship.
Strongs Concordance Hebrew Chaldees Dictionary, word #7812

There are many scriptures like this that are going to astound you which the Holy Spirit will show you, however Psalms 29 and Psalms 96 *are going to be more than enough now to give us the keys we need to expose the truth.* It will allow the people of God to approach the Lord the acceptable way and to make way for God's presence to fall as never before.

Notice in Psalms 29 – Hebrew translation verse 1 and 2 – Say we must render to our God who is called Hashem the honor and might due his name. How? *By bowing down, not only with our hearts but with our bodies, in the beauty of holiness.* It is *saying we honor God by bowing down or* of course by kneeling or prostrating ourselves in the beauty of holiness. Holiness is beautiful to God and to us as priests we must, we must, we must obey God's commandments.

And the true love of God is this - that we obey his commandments. 1st John 5:3

The Lord further says – Be Holy as I am Holy. Holiness is a prerequisite for the priesthood. The priests who were with Aaron and his sons were ordered to have a crown on their heads, which were engraved with the words *Holiness unto the Lord.* We must study the word and then *obey* it. God has exalted his word above his name. The requirement for all priests is that we are to be holy. Before worship, we must always cleanse ourselves in the blood of Jesus. We must repent of anything whether by imagination or act that is unholy if we are to be acceptable to the Lord. If our offerings of worship are to be pleasing we must be totally honest and transparent before the Lord. *Otherwise, don't waste your time.* Without true repentance, without honesty to the Lord, there cannot be forgiveness.

So then notice, we give honor to God by bowing, kneeling, or prostrating oneself before God in the beauty of holiness.

The time is coming and indeed has already come when the true worshippers will worship the Father in spirit and in truth (reality) and the Father seeks such worshipers. John 4:23

5

ARE WE FRIGID LOVERS OF GOD?

If you notice in the earlier scriptures of Revelations chapter 4, the four living creatures and the 24 elders are prostrating themselves in worship before the Lord in the Holy of Holies. *Nobody is standing. Nothing stands or sits in the presence of the Lord in the Holy of Holies.* No spiritual being and certainly not flesh. However, once again, if you take a look at our church services today most of the priests (people) are standing during worship. Many sit and only a few bow, kneel, or prostrate.

This is totally outrageous! During our worship we have entered the heavenly realm of worship because the scripture says we enter boldly into the Holy of Holies by the Blood of the Lamb. We are actually in the throne room at the feet of the Father, the Son, the Holy Spirit, the four living creatures, angels, and the twenty-four elders. We are totally out of place when we stand or sit. When we stand or sit in the throne room it is a total disrespect of the Lord. It is an embarrassment to God before the angels of the heavens. Let me repeat again. *Nobody, but nobody stands or sits in the Holy of*

Please take note if somebody has a problem with their legs and cannot kneel or bow, there is no condemnation. Your grace and favor is as much as somebody who physically can. However, you do want to pray that God will heal the conditions so you can bow.

NO FLESH STANDS IN THE HOLY OF HOLIES

Holies! Open your spiritual eyes and read Revelations 4 and 5 (and the rest of Revelations) over and over until it is in your spirit. Glory, strength, splendor, power, majesty, and holiness are his, and only his. Let no man or woman share that glory. Yet believe it or not we attempt to. How? We honor God the same way we honor men.

If the president of the United States walked into the church we would probably all stand up and clap. Which, of course, would be correct. Give honor where honor is due. Why would we not bow down? Naturally, because he is *NOT GOD*.

That is precisely the point. Bowing, kneeling, and prostrating is *reserved for God!* We are to respect each other as brothers and sisters. We are to respect our pastors. We would not blow bubbles of chewing gum in front of a pastor while he's talking to us. We would never be rude or disrespectful because we are to respect men of God who have been put in these positions.

How much more is the God of Israel and his Holy Son to be reverenced? Standing and sitting has been a tradition in the church for centuries during worship. The Jews brought their man-made traditions into religion as well. These traditions have nothing to do with God. They are merely a dead ritualistic form created by man – not God.

As Jesus said, The time is coming and indeed has already come when the true worshippers will worship the Father in spirit and in truth (reality) the Father seeks such worshippers. John 4:23

In truth, meaning knowing God is truly in front of us as we worship. He is seeing everything, hearing each and every word we sing. He is aware of our heart-condition as far as our attitude in which we are offering to him our adoration. Truth also meaning that there is no entrance into the Holy of Holies, except by the blood of the Messiah and Savior Jesus Christ.

In the spirit meaning, God is a spirit and has to be worshiped as such. His ways are far above our ways, therefore we must be careful to follow the leading of the Holy Spirit, which will always be confirmed by the word of God. God has a specific pattern. *We must follow it, and not man's way.*

To stand in the Holy of Holies is an abomination! This is an affront to the Lord. We cannot continue to honor God the same way as man. *The word is worship and the original Hebrew meaning is to bow down, kneel down, or prostrate oneself.* This is the way the priests of the Body of Christ must worship when they are in the Holy of Holies.

What we bind on earth must be bound in heaven. Matthew 18:18

In other words what is declared illegal and unacceptable on earth has to be illegal and unacceptable in heaven. Standing or sitting in the Holy of Holies before God the Father, the Son, and the Holy Spirit along with the angels of Heaven and the four living creatures and twenty-four elders is definitely illegal and unacceptable worship.

Prostrating, kneeling, or bowing is the manifestation of your inner heart condition or your relationship that you have with God. Is he truly God, the Lord God Almighty, Creator of Heaven and Earth? Is he truly our Lord who we submit to with consent? Is he truly our all in all or do we share him with other God's in our life as the Israelites did in the Old Testament? Have we given ourselves in true love intimacy to him or our we more like frigid lovers to him? Are we really honored to belong to him or are we ashamed of him before men? Are we truly devoted to him as priests or are we more concerned what people think of us? Are we still filled with poisonous pride in our hearts or have we died like a kernel of wheat that has fallen to the ground and been resurrected to new life? Dead to self and alive to Christ! Do we truly realize we can do nothing without our precious God and our precious Savior Jesus Christ or are we still putting ourselves together on the throne with him eagerly seeking man's adulation and adoration? Are we willing to submit to his commandments and be holy as he is holy or do we still make excuses?

When we humbly bow down, kneel down, or prostrate ourselves with a pure heart in worship service, we are really making a statement of where we stand with the Lord before ourselves, other men, and the Lord Himself. It is truly the highest point of intimacy we can have with the Lord. In the garden of Gesemane at Jesus' most vulnerable point he threw himself on the ground before the Father putting himself completely in his hands and at his mercy.

Sickness and disease must bow to the Father and the Son. Every demonic spirit bows before the Lord. Death bows at the name of Jesus. All heaven bows before him. Will we? Not just when we feel like it, but every time we come into his presence in the Holy of Holies.

6

WE MUST UPROOT, TEAR DOWN, AND REPLANT OUR WORSHIP

We must respond to the Holy Spirit or we are resisting him! *We must change the order of our worship services to make it acceptable to the Lord.*

If we want to see the glory fall like heavy rain in our lives and in our church this is the time to submit to the Holy Spirit. The Lord wants to come to his people, but now he's saying to us, we must approach him the correct and priestly way. David had to learn this the hard way as we mentioned before. He wanted the presence of God so badly. He had good intentions, but his mistake was he tried to carry the Ark on the oxen cart. *The Lord is saying NO.* God has a priestly way. God has a heavenly way. God has his own unique pattern of doing things. We too are trying to carry his presence on an oxen cart by standing in his presence instead of kneeling. He says *no* to David and now *no* to us. *Do not carry my presence and glory on an oxen cart. I want you to carry it on your shoulders. As you carry my glory and presence, which is WEIGHTY, on your shoulders. You will find my presence and glory causing you to kneel, bow, and finally to prostrate yourself to the ground. Then I will press you right where you are and the oil of my anointing will flow like a river from you.*

The worship we offer now in our churches is "strange fire", "strange worship", or in Hebrew "alien fire".

The sons of Aaron the priest offered wrong type of worship to the Lord. They meant well. However man's ways are not good enough for the Lord. They put fire in their censors and put incense on it and offered it to the Lord. God called this strange and unholy fire because he did not command it.

Verse 2: *And then came forth fire from before the Lord and killed them, and they died before the Lord.*

Verse 3: *Then Moses said to Aaron, This is what the Lord meant when he said, I (and my will, not their own) will be acknowledged as hallowed by those who come near me; and before all the people I will be honored and Aaron said nothing.* Leviticus 10:1-3

You shall make a distinction and recognize a difference between the holy and the common or unholy, and between the unclean and the clean. Leviticus 10:10

The Holy Spirit is telling us in these verses that if we intend as priests to come close to the Lord, we must treat what is holy, holy and not common, and the Lord must be honored in the highest way possible before men in worship. Our way is not good enough. It is His way and only His way that is right. As Jesus always said, Not my will, but your will Lord.

Remember our pattern of worship must match the heavenly pattern!

Remember when we pray, we seek him, *when we worship, he seeks us.* God is seeking worshippers who approach him in a heavenly priestly manner. It is no longer good enough just to sing songs. We must sing and worship at his feet, to both the Father and the Son. Sing and worship to our Father who is unseen. Yes, do not be fooled into thinking he is not there. Jesus already tells us to go into our secret place to pray to our Father who is *unseen* (in secret) but make no mistake. He, His Son, and the Holy Spirit are there waiting for us in the Holy of Holies to fill our hearts and theirs with joy.

As we enter into this true experience of worship we cannot help but kneel down, bow down, or prostrate ourselves before the Living God whether it's in a private place or in front of the whole church in public worship. What's the difference? How can we see anything else but his glory, no matter where we are?

Bowing, kneeling, and prostrating consummates the covenant agreement with God.

Isn't it interesting when Satan came to tempt Jesus?

And he said to him, These things are taken together, I will give you. If you will prostrate yourself before me and do homage and worship me. Matthew 4:9

As we read this the Holy Spirit makes it very clear that this represented a very important and serious act of the body and heart that Satan desired. He wanted the Son of God to perform this act. Obviously Satan did not think of this on his own.

He watched the Father and Son be worshiped like this countless times. This was the perfect order. The Perfect Heavenly Pattern. The Perfect Divine Will of God.

The Holy Spirit wants us to understand that this true pattern of priestly worship is equivalent to a bride and groom finally, after taking marriage vows and agreeing to the words of the marriage covenant, making love together. This consummates the marriage and seals the covenant. This consummation only involves these two people. Their spirits, their souls, and their bodies become one intertwined. Two literally become one. It is true intimacy.

It is the same with kneeling, bowing, and prostrating in worship. We have made a covenant with the Lord by his word. As the bride and the groom speak together, we also speak with our Lord together. However when we move towards worship in these yielded worship positions we are literally spiritually consummating a very intimate relationship between the Lord and ourselves. We are pledging ourselves in love and passion very intimately. This goes much more deeply than we can ever understand.

This process, this spiritual intercourse between the creator and creation will produce a oneness that is beyond all human understanding. Now can you understand why Satan so much coveted this act of prostration from Jesus. God's glory and presence will be poured out without measure upon those who desire him more than anything else during these times of worship. Ignorance Versus Stubbornness and Pride.

It is one thing not to have knowledge of something and do something that is not correct in the sight of the Lord.

It is another to have the knowledge and then continue to do what is wrong. This is called stubbornness and pride. Stubbornness is as the sin of witchcraft. The question is, are we willing to submit to the leading of the Holy Spirit. Do we have a teachable spirit?

One of the earliest cases of disobedience towards the Lord in the area of worship came in Genesis 4:2, which is the story about Cain and Abel. Please pay attention. Abel was a keeper of *SHEEP*. But Cain was a tiller of the ground. In time Cain gave an offering to the Lord from the fruit of the ground.

Abel offered to the Lord the firstborn of his flock.

And the Lord had respect and regard for Abel and for his offering. Verse 5 But for Cain and his offering he had no respect or regard. Genesis 4:4-5

So Cain was exceedingly angry and indignant, and he looked sad, depressed, and dejected. The problem with Cain's offering was in Genesis 3:17 God tells Adam because of his disobedience the ground is under a curse. In other words the offering or worship that Cain offered was under a curse. It was strange fire, unholy fire, and wrong worship.

Now this is where the problem arose.

The Lord said to Cain, Why are you angry? And why do you look sad and dejected? Verse 7 If you do well, will you not be accepted? And if you do not do well, sin crouches at your door; it's desire is for you, but you must master it. Genesis 4:6-7

Of course, we know the end. Immediately after God spoke to Cain, he went to Abel and killed him out of jealousy, pride, and disobedience. The result was the worst thing that could happen to Cain.

Verse 16: So Cain went away from the presence of the Lord.

Note that Cain's offering was out of ignorance as our worship is out of ignorance. As discussed before, only the original Hebrew interpretation clearly in detail denotes worship as bowing down, kneeling, and prostrating oneself. King James Version uses only the general term worship, which is not specific enough.

After Cain offered his unacceptable offering and worship God gently and clearly explained to him how to make the correction. God's nature is loving kindness, tenderhearted mercy, unfailing love and faithfulness.

However Cain was not willing to obey. Again his jealousy over Abel, pride, stubbornness to obey and disobedience led to his killing his brother Able as well as *never being able to come close to God.*

We can learn much from Cain. We can avoid our downfall by being teachable.

Exalt Hashem, our God, and bow at his footstool; He is Holy.
Verse 9 - Exalt Hashem, Our God, and bow at his Holy Mountain;
for holy is Hashem Our God. Psalms 99:5, 9 Original Hebrew Translation

7

GOD IS CALLING YOU
TO COME CLOSE TO HIM

It is no accident you are reading this...
Nothing is an accident in the life of a Christian

God wants you to draw close to Him. He wants to draw close to
you with intimacy, such intense intimacy that you have never experienced before. He wants to manifest his tangible presence. Not
from afar, but at his feet. He wants to release the weight of his glory
upon you and the entire church. *His season is now.* Are you going
to be Abel whose heart is soft and pliable or Cain who is going to
resist the Holy Spirit and never attain his real presence? We already
have the perfect sacrifice. The perfect sacrificial lamb to offer God,
which is Jesus.

However we must approach God his way all the time. Not only
you as an individual but the entire Body of Christ and that will be
divided up into each individual church.

When God is moving extreme changes are going to happen. One
of the first things that happen is the Lord shows us the things that
are not right in our lives. Get rid of it quickly. Burn it at the altar.

It's cancer to you. It's poisonous. Don't play with it – *it will kill you in the presence of God.* Maybe it's unforgiveness, resentment, or bitterness towards someone. Burn it. When you accepted Christ *you lost your license to hate*, to be bitter, and to be resentful. You have been purchased by the Lord. You are not your own anymore. Burn it at the altar or it will kill you!

Maybe it's lust, lying, greed, or pride - it does not matter. Repent of it. As you bow down before the Lord in worship he will supernaturally exchange his nature for yours. Continually cleanse yourself in the Blood of Christ when coming before him. Obey what he is telling you to do. This is acceptable worship. This is what he is pleased with.

Humble yourself under the mighty hand of God and in due time he will exalt you. I Peter 5:6

You may be thinking, everything is fine for me – why should I change? The only thing that keeps us from getting what is par – excellent is by accepting what is good. Once you taste and see that the glory and true presence of God is irreplaceable, you will never settle for the *lukewarmness* again. If you are a pastor or worship leader you may be content with your service on Sunday. Everything is comfortable. Everything has its tidy order of things. Everything is fine. **No it's not fine!** God wants to come in and change things. He wants to release his river of life that flow from the throne of God and from the Lamb of God. This river is for the healing of the nations. It is for the healing of us that we may be the bride that Christ expects to have. You must be willing to change and seek his face, not religion.

Intimacy with us is what the Lord desires most.

The Holy Spirit is telling us now that the Father had to see His Beloved Son be torn apart on a cross and be offered up as a sacrifice for us. Why? So that we could be cleansed from our sins and come close to him. Think about this. The Father desires so much to have intimacy with us that he was willing to see his Son be tortured. How the Father loves us and is jealous for us.

As a matter of fact, we can see with our own eyes how desperate and anxious Father God was for extreme intimacy with us.

In three different gospels we will see the exact same account of what transpired as Jesus died on the cross.

And Jesus cried again with a loud voice and gave up his spirit.
Verse 51: *And at once the curtain of the sanctuary of the temple was torn in two from top to bottom; the earth shook and the rocks were split.* Matthew 27:50-51

And Jesus uttered a loud cry, and breathed out his life.
Verse 38: *And the curtain (of the Holy of Holies) of the temple was torn in two from top to bottom.* Mark 16:37-38

It was now about the sixth hour (midday) and darkness enveloped the whole land and earth until the ninth hour (about three o'clock in the afternoon).
Verse 45: *While the sun's light faded or was darkened; and the curtain (of the Holy of Holies) of the temple was torn in two.*
Verse 46: *And Jesus crying out with a loud voice said, Father into your hands I commit my spirit! And with these words, He expired.*
Luke 23:44-46

All of these accounts say the exact same thing. Immediately after Jesus died, the curtain of the Holy of Holies was torn apart by God himself.

We all know that before Jesus died only one priest from the whole nation of Israel could enter the Holy of Holies to have this close intimacy with God.

At the point of Jesus dying, the one statement that God was telling all mankind was, I have been waiting so long for this moment. Now I can embrace all of my children who come to me. They don't have to be afraid to come too close to me. As a matter of fact I *want them to come so close that they can feel my heartbeat and smell my fragrance.* I dearly want to be called their Father and I will call them my children. I have made the way for you by tearing the curtain in two. I love you so much that I was willing to watch my only Begotten Son suffer in a way that was unbearable to me, however my love for you was so great that I accepted my Son's sacrifice for you, just to have you as my very own.

35

Seeing now how the Lord wants his people to come close, *we must all learn the acceptable way to enter his Holy presence.*

The season is now for us to drop what we are doing and come near to him, not tomorrow, today. The Holy Spirit is telling us that worship, supernaturally brings intimacy. Worship, which is true priestly, heavenly worship, not man's preconceived ideas. We have learned already the Hebrew word – שָׁחָה shâchâh. It means to bow, kneel, and prostrate oneself. *Not only in heart, but also bodily.* Again, most places you see the word worship in the King James Version does not read worship in the original Hebrew. Again, in the Tenach, which is the Old Testament in Hebrew with the English translation it reads – bow down, kneel, and prostrate. That is what true worship is. Again – not only in heart, but also bodily.

The Lord is calling you to come close but you must approach him as a heavenly priest. True worship is true intimacy with him. Intimacy is when two hearts become one. When the final wall of separation is torn down and manifested in reality. When there is true transparency between us, the Father, the Son, and Holy Spirit. When there are no hidden thoughts that are kept from one another. When truth and affection are shared between the Lord and us.

Intimacy is the most intense part of a relationship. Intimacy is the only true place where God's love can be manifested. It is in this place, says the Lord, My love, My nature, and My life can flow from me through you. This is the place I want to share with my children who are my priests. The veil of the temple was torn so that I could invite my people into a true intimate relationship with me.

Then I saw another angel flying in mid-air with an eternal gospel (good news) to tell the inhabitants of the earth, to every race, tribe, language, and people.
Verse 7: *And he cried with a mighty voice. Revere God and give Him glory (honor and praise in worship) for the hour of his judgement has arrived. **Fall down before Him; pay homage, adoration and worship Him** who created Heaven and Earth, the sea, and the springs (fountains) of water.* Revelations 14:6-7

Seeing the above two verses says it all. The angel in a loud voice announces to the inhabitants of the world. Revere God, fall down before him, pay homage adoration, and worship him. We as children of God have been instructed to preach this to the world. *Before we do this, the church must do it ourselves.* We must repent and turn from our lukewarm dead formalistic ways of worshipping in the Holy of Holies in the church and get on our knees, bow down, or prostrate ourselves to the Lord. We must declare to ourselves to the Lord and to the world that our God reigns. That Jesus who was raised from the lowest part of the Earth to the highest part of Heaven has been exalted at the right hand of God. Not only in words but also in our actions!

Jesus said to the Samaritan Woman –"You Samaritans worship but don't know who you worship." John 4:22

Should we ask ourselves the question, do we really know who we worship? As we watch millions of Muslims worship Allah the false god, notice how they all bow down. At the very least, this should bring us to an awareness that the very one who loves us, the very one who protects us, the very one who saved us by watching his precious Son die on the cross, the very one who truly created Heaven and Earth and us, is he not worthy to bow before in worship, not only in heart, but body?

Not just when we feel like it, but each and every time we enter into the Holy of Holies. This is how heaven worships him and this is how his church must worship him. "On Earth as it is in Heaven."

ISAIAH 66:18-24 **THE TENACH**

and the mouse will all be consumed together — the word of HASHEM.
¹⁸ I [know] their actions and their thoughts; [the time] has come to gather all the nations and tongues, * they will come and see My glory. ¹⁹ I will put a sign upon them and send some of them as survivors* to the nations — Tarshish, Pul, Lud, the Archers, Tubal and Javan, the distant islands who have not heard of My fame and not seen My glory — and they will declare My glory among the nations. ²⁰ They will bring all your brethren from all the nations as an offering to HASHEM — with horses and with chariots and with covered wagons and with mules — with joyous dances, to My holy mountain, Jerusalem, says HASHEM; just as the Children of Israel bring the offering in a pure vessel to the House of HASHEM. ²¹ From them, too, I will take men to be Kohanim and Levites, * says HASHEM. ²² For just as the new heavens and the new earth that I will make will endure before Me — the word of HASHEM — so will your offspring and your name endure. ²³ It shall be that at every New Moon and on every Sabbath all mankind will come to prostrate themselves before Me, says HASHEM. ²⁴ And they will go out and see the corpses of the men who rebelled against Me, for their decay will not cease and their fire* will not be extinguished, and they will lie in disgrace before all mankind.

* It shall be that at every New Moon and on every Sabbath
all mankind will come to prostrate themselves before Me, says HASHEM.

נביאים אחרונים ישעיה

יח וְהֶעָכְבָּר יַחְדָּו יָסֻפוּ נְאֻם־יהוה: וְאָנֹכִי מַעֲשֵׂיהֶם וּמַחְשְׁבֹתֵיהֶם בָּאָה
יט לְקַבֵּץ אֶת־כָּל־הַגּוֹיִם וְהַלְּשֹׁנוֹת וּבָאוּ וְרָאוּ אֶת־כְּבוֹדִי: וְשַׂמְתִּי בָהֶם
אוֹת וְשִׁלַּחְתִּי מֵהֶם ׀ פְּלֵיטִים אֶל־הַגּוֹיִם תַּרְשִׁישׁ פּוּל וְלוּד מֹשְׁכֵי קֶשֶׁת
תֻּבַל וְיָוָן הָאִיִּים הָרְחֹקִים אֲשֶׁר לֹא־שָׁמְעוּ אֶת־שִׁמְעִי וְלֹא־רָאוּ אֶת־
כ כְּבוֹדִי וְהִגִּידוּ אֶת־כְּבוֹדִי בַּגּוֹיִם: וְהֵבִיאוּ אֶת־כָּל־אֲחֵיכֶם מִכָּל־הַגּוֹיִם ׀
מִנְחָה ׀ לַיהוה בַּסּוּסִים וּבָרֶכֶב וּבַצַּבִּים וּבַפְּרָדִים וּבַכִּרְכָּרוֹת עַל הַר
קָדְשִׁי יְרוּשָׁלַם אָמַר יהוה כַּאֲשֶׁר יָבִיאוּ בְנֵי יִשְׂרָאֵל אֶת־הַמִּנְחָה בִּכְלִי
כא-כב טָהוֹר בֵּית יהוה: וְגַם־מֵהֶם אֶקַּח לַכֹּהֲנִים לַלְוִיִּם אָמַר יהוה: כִּי כַאֲשֶׁר
הַשָּׁמַיִם הַחֲדָשִׁים וְהָאָרֶץ הַחֲדָשָׁה אֲשֶׁר אֲנִי עֹשֶׂה עֹמְדִים לְפָנַי נְאֻם־
כג יהוה כֵּן יַעֲמֹד זַרְעֲכֶם וְשִׁמְכֶם: וְהָיָה מִדֵּי־חֹדֶשׁ בְּחָדְשׁוֹ וּמִדֵּי שַׁבָּת
כד בְּשַׁבַּתּוֹ יָבוֹא כָל־בָּשָׂר לְהִשְׁתַּחֲוֹת לְפָנַי אָמַר יהוה: וְיָצְאוּ וְרָאוּ בְּפִגְרֵי
הָאֲנָשִׁים הַפֹּשְׁעִים בִּי כִּי תוֹלַעְתָּם לֹא תָמוּת וְאִשָּׁם לֹא תִכְבֶּה וְהָיוּ
דֵרָאוֹן לְכָל־בָּשָׂר:

וְהָיָה מִדֵּי־חֹדֶשׁ בְּחָדְשׁוֹ וּמִדֵּי שַׁבָּת בְּשַׁבַּתּוֹ
יָבוֹא כָל־בָּשָׂר לְהִשְׁתַּחֲוֹת לְפָנַי אָמַר יהוה:

סכום הפסוקים של ישעיה אלף ומאתים ותשעים וחמשה. אמת ארצה סימן. בריח ניחח ארצה אתכם סימן.

38

When He favors the righteous and rejects those unmindful of Him, God assists man in remaining on His chosen path. Your Holy Sanctuary. ³ Do not cause me to be drawn with the wicked and with the doers of iniquity, who speak peace with their companions though evil is in their hearts. ⁴ Give them according to their deeds and according to the evil of their actions; according to their handiwork give them, render their recompense to them. ⁵ For they do not contemplate the deeds of HASHEM or His handiwork; may He tear them down and not rebuild them. ⁶ Blessed is HASHEM, for He has heard° the sound of my supplications. ⁷ HASHEM is my strength and my shield, in Him my heart trusted and I was helped; and my heart exulted, with my song I praise Him: ⁸ "HASHEM is strength to them; and the stronghold of salvations for His anointed is He." ⁹ Save Your nation, and bless Your inheritance; tend them and elevate them forever.

29 *God's power and glory pervade all of creation. It functions solely according to His will, as has been manifested by His intervention in history.* ¹ A psalm of David: Render unto HASHEM, you sons of the powerful, ° render unto HASHEM honor and might. ² Render unto HASHEM the honor due His Name, bow to HASHEM in the beauty of holiness. ³ The voice of HASHEM is upon the waters, the God of Glory thunders; HASHEM is upon vast waters. ⁴ The voice of HASHEM [comes] in power! The voice of HASHEM [comes] in majesty! ⁵ The voice of HASHEM breaks the cedars, HASHEM shatters the cedars of Lebanon! ⁶ He makes them prance about like a calf; Lebanon and Siryon like young re'eimim. ° ⁷ The voice of HASHEM cleaves with shafts of fire. ° ⁸ The voice·of HASHEM convulses the wilderness; HASHEM convulses the wilderness of Kadesh. ° ⁹ The voice of HASHEM frightens the hinds, and strips the forests bare; while in His Temple all will proclaim, "Glory!" ¹⁰ HASHEM sat enthroned at the Flood; ° HASHEM sits enthroned as King forever. ¹¹ HASHEM will give might to His nation, HASHEM will bless His nation with peace.

30 *As darkness precedes dawn, so travail should be accepted as a prerequisite for success.* ¹ A psalm, a song for the inauguration of the Temple, by David. ² I will exalt You, HASHEM, for You have drawn me up, and not let my foes rejoice over me. ³ HASHEM, my God, I cried out to You and You healed me. ⁴ HASHEM, You have raised up my soul from the lower world; ° You have preserved me from my descent to the pit. ⁵ Sing to HASHEM, His devout ones, and give thanks to His holy Name. ⁶ For His anger endures but a moment; life results from His favor. In the evening one lies down weeping, but with dawn — a cry of joy! ⁷ I had said in my serenity, "I would never falter." ⁸ But, HASHEM, all is through Your favor — You supported my greatness with might; should You but conceal Your face, I would be confounded. ⁹ To You, HASHEM, I would call and to the Lord I would appeal. ¹⁰ What gain is there in my death, in my descent to the pit? Will the. dust acknowledge You? Will it declare Your truth? ¹¹ Hear, HASHEM, and favor me; HASHEM, be my Helper! ¹² You have transformed my lament into dancing for me, You undid my sackcloth and girded me with gladness. ¹³ So that my soul might sing to You and not be stilled, HASHEM, my God, forever will I thank You.

31 ¹ For the conductor, a song by David. ² In You, HASHEM, I have taken refuge, ° let me not be shamed ever; in Your righteousness liberate me. ³ Incline to me Your ear, quickly rescue me; be for me a stronghold rock, a fortress to save me. ⁴ For my Rock and my Fortress are You, for Your Name's sake guide me and lead me. ⁵ Remove me from this net that they have hidden for me, for You are my stronghold. ⁶ In Your hand I entrust my spirit; You redeemed

were betrayed to Saul, and time and again God rescued him (see *I Samuel* Chs. 22-24).

כתובים · תהלים

ג דְּבִיר קָדְשֶׁךָ: אַל־תִּמְשְׁכֵנִי עִם־רְשָׁעִים וְעִם־פֹּעֲלֵי אָוֶן דֹּבְרֵי שָׁלוֹם עִם־
ד רֵעֵיהֶם וְרָעָה בִּלְבָבָם: תֶּן־לָהֶם כְּפָעֳלָם וּכְרֹעַ מַעַלְלֵיהֶם כְּמַעֲשֵׂה יְדֵיהֶם
ה תֵּן לָהֶם הָשֵׁב גְּמוּלָם לָהֶם: כִּי לֹא יָבִינוּ אֶל־פְּעֻלֹּת יהוה וְאֶל־מַעֲשֵׂה
ו־ז יָדָיו יֶהֶרְסֵם וְלֹא יִבְנֵם: בָּרוּךְ יהוה כִּי־שָׁמַע קוֹל תַּחֲנוּנָי: יהוה ו עֻזִּי וּמָגִנִּי
ח בּוֹ בָטַח לִבִּי וְנֶעֱזָרְתִּי וַיַּעֲלֹז לִבִּי וּמִשִּׁירִי אֲהוֹדֶנּוּ: יהוה עֹז־לָמוֹ וּמָעוֹז
ט יְשׁוּעוֹת מְשִׁיחוֹ הוּא: הוֹשִׁיעָה ו אֶת־עַמֶּךָ וּבָרֵךְ אֶת־נַחֲלָתֶךָ וּרְעֵם
וְנַשְּׂאֵם עַד־הָעוֹלָם:

כט
ה ה לחרש
א־ב מִזְמוֹר לְדָוִד הָבוּ לַיהוה בְּנֵי אֵלִים הָבוּ לַיהוה כָּבוֹד וָעֹז: הָבוּ לַיהוה
ג כְּבוֹד שְׁמוֹ הִשְׁתַּחֲווּ לַיהוה בְּהַדְרַת־קֹדֶשׁ: קוֹל יהוה עַל־הַמָּיִם אֵל־
ד הַכָּבוֹד הִרְעִים יהוה עַל־מַיִם רַבִּים: קוֹל־יהוה בַּכֹּחַ קוֹל יהוה בֶּהָדָר:
ה־ו קוֹל יהוה שֹׁבֵר אֲרָזִים וַיְשַׁבֵּר יהוה אֶת־אַרְזֵי הַלְּבָנוֹן: וַיַּרְקִידֵם כְּמוֹ־עֵגֶל
ז־ח לְבָנוֹן וְשִׂרְיֹן כְּמוֹ בֶן־רְאֵמִים: קוֹל־יהוה חֹצֵב לַהֲבוֹת אֵשׁ: קוֹל יהוה
ט יָחִיל מִדְבָּר יָחִיל יהוה מִדְבַּר קָדֵשׁ: קוֹל יהוה ו יְחוֹלֵל אַיָּלוֹת וַיֶּחֱשֹׂף
י יְעָרוֹת וּבְהֵיכָלוֹ כֻּלּוֹ אֹמֵר כָּבוֹד: יהוה לַמַּבּוּל יָשָׁב וַיֵּשֶׁב יהוה מֶלֶךְ
יא לְעוֹלָם: יהוה עֹז לְעַמּוֹ יִתֵּן יהוה ו יְבָרֵךְ אֶת־עַמּוֹ בַשָּׁלוֹם:

ל
יום שני
א־ב מִזְמוֹר שִׁיר־חֲנֻכַּת הַבַּיִת לְדָוִד: אֲרוֹמִמְךָ יהוה כִּי דִלִּיתָנִי וְלֹא־שִׂמַּחְתָּ
ג־ד אֹיְבַי לִי: יהוה אֱלֹהָי שִׁוַּעְתִּי אֵלֶיךָ וַתִּרְפָּאֵנִי: יהוה הֶעֱלִיתָ מִן־שְׁאוֹל
ה נַפְשִׁי חִיִּיתַנִי °מִיָּורְדִי [°מִיָּרְדִי ק] בוֹר: זַמְּרוּ לַיהוה חֲסִידָיו וְהוֹדוּ
ו לְזֵכֶר קָדְשׁוֹ: כִּי רֶגַע ו בְּאַפּוֹ חַיִּים בִּרְצוֹנוֹ בָּעֶרֶב יָלִין בֶּכִי וְלַבֹּקֶר רִנָּה:
ז־ח וַאֲנִי אָמַרְתִּי בְשַׁלְוִי בַּל־אֶמּוֹט לְעוֹלָם: יהוה בִּרְצוֹנְךָ הֶעֱמַדְתָּה לְהַרְרִי
ט עֹז הִסְתַּרְתָּ פָנֶיךָ הָיִיתִי נִבְהָל: אֵלֶיךָ יהוה אֶקְרָא וְאֶל־אֲדֹנָי אֶתְחַנָּן: מַה־
י בֶּצַע בְּדָמִי בְּרִדְתִּי אֶל־שָׁחַת הֲיוֹדְךָ עָפָר הֲיַגִּיד אֲמִתֶּךָ: שְׁמַע־יהוה
יא־יב וְחָנֵּנִי יהוה הֱיֵה־עֹזֵר לִי: הָפַכְתָּ מִסְפְּדִי לְמָחוֹל לִי פִּתַּחְתָּ שַׂקִּי וַתְּאַזְּרֵנִי
יג שִׂמְחָה: לְמַעַן ו יְזַמֶּרְךָ כָבוֹד וְלֹא יִדֹּם יהוה אֱלֹהַי לְעוֹלָם אוֹדֶךָּ:

לא
א־ב לַמְנַצֵּחַ מִזְמוֹר לְדָוִד: בְּךָ־יהוה חָסִיתִי אַל־אֵבוֹשָׁה לְעוֹלָם בְּצִדְקָתְךָ
ג פַלְּטֵנִי: הַטֵּה אֵלַי ו אָזְנְךָ מְהֵרָה הַצִּילֵנִי הֱיֵה לִי ו לְצוּר־מָעוֹז לְבֵית מְצוּדוֹת
ד לְהוֹשִׁיעֵנִי: כִּי־סַלְעִי וּמְצוּדָתִי אָתָּה וּלְמַעַן שִׁמְךָ תַּנְחֵנִי וּתְנַהֲלֵנִי:
ה תּוֹצִיאֵנִי מֵרֶשֶׁת זוּ טָמְנוּ לִי כִּי־אַתָּה מָעוּזִּי: בְּיָדְךָ אַפְקִיד רוּחִי פָּדִיתָה

28:6. Such was David's trust that he speaks as if he had already been answered (Meiri).

29:1. Abraham, Isaac, and Jacob, who were "powerful" in their righteousness.

29:6. See 22:22.

29:7. When God pronounced the Ten Commandments, the very words sprang forth like fire, so to speak, and seared their way into the Tablets of the Law (Midrash).

29:8. "Kadesh," cognate with kadosh, "holy," is another name for the Wilderness of Sinai, where Israel became

sanctified by accepting the Torah.

29:10. In Messianic times God's reign will be as absolute as it was during the Flood, when nearly all life was washed away.

30:4. The flames of frustration, anguish, and melancholy are the equivalent of the fires of Gehinnom, "the netherworld." Thus, the Talmud (Nedarim 22a) teaches, "Whoever becomes angry is subjected to all types of Gehinnom" (R' Yerucham Levovitz).

31:2. David composed this psalm while in flight from Saul's relentless pursuit. Time and again his whereabouts *innocent they condemn.* [22] *Then HASHEM became a stronghold for me, and my God, the Rock of my refuge.* [23] *He turned upon them their own violence, and with their own evil He will cut them off; HASHEM, our God, will cut them off.*

95

Come acknowledge God as Creator and guiding force of the universe. Do not emulate your ancestors who strayed after falsehood.

[1] Come! Let us sing to HASHEM, let us call out to the Rock of our salvation. [2] Let us greet Him with thanksgiving, with praiseful songs let us call out to Him. [3] For a great God is HASHEM, and a great King above all heavenly powers. [4] For in His power are the hidden mysteries of earth, and the mountain summits are His. [5] For His is the sea and He perfected it, and the dry land — His hands fashioned it. [6] Come! Let us prostrate ourselves and bow, let us kneel before God, our Maker. [7] For He is our God and we can be the flock He pastures, and the sheep in His charge — even today, if we but heed His call! [8] Do not harden your heart as at Meribah,* as on the day of Massah* in the Wilderness; [9] when Your ancestors tried Me; they tested Me, though they had seen My deed. [10] For forty years I was angry with the generation; then I said, "An errant-hearted people are they, and they know not My ways." [11] Therefore, I have sworn in My anger that they shall not enter My land of contentment.

96

When all the nations on earth will recognize God's sovereignty, they will join in a new song acknowledging Him.

[1] Sing to HASHEM a new song; sing to HASHEM, everyone on earth. [2] Sing to HASHEM, bless His Name; announce His salvation daily. [3] Relate His glory among the nations; among all peoples, His wonders: [4] That HASHEM is great and exceedingly lauded; awesome is He above all heavenly powers. [5] For all the gods of the peoples are nothings — but HASHEM made heaven! [6] Glory and majesty are before Him, might and splendor in His Sanctuary. [7] Render unto HASHEM, O families of the peoples, render unto HASHEM honor and might. [8] Render unto HASHEM honor worthy of His Name; take an offering and come to His courtyards. [9] Prostrate yourselves before HASHEM in His intensely holy place; tremble before Him, everyone on earth. [10] Declare among the nations, "HASHEM has reigned!" Indeed, the world is fixed so that it cannot falter. He will judge the peoples with fairness. [11] The heavens will be glad and the earth will rejoice,* the sea and its fullness will roar; [12] the field and everything in it will exult; then all the trees of the forest will sing with joy — [13] before HASHEM, for He will have arrived, He will have arrived to judge the earth. He will judge the world with righteousness, and peoples with His truth.

97

After the upheavals that will precede the Messiah's coming, the world will recognize its folly, and God will reign supreme over the entire earth.

[1] HASHEM has reigned,* let the world rejoice; let the numerous islands be glad. [2] Cloud and dense darkness surround Him;* righteousness and justice are His throne's foundation. [3] Fire goes before Him and consumes His enemies all around. [4] His lightning bolts lit up the world, [the inhabitants of] the earth saw and tremble. [5] Mountains* melted like wax before HASHEM, before the Lord of all the earth. [6] The heavens declare His righteousness, and all the peoples saw His glory. [7] Humiliated will be all who worship idols, who pride themselves in worthless gods; bow to Him, all you powers. [8] Zion heard and was glad, and the daughters of Judah exulted, because of Your judgments, HASHEM. [9] For You, HASHEM, are supreme above all the earth; exceedingly exalted above all powers. [10] O lovers of HASHEM, despise evil! He guards the lives of His devout ones, from the hand of the wicked He rescues them. [11] Light is sown for the righteous; and for the upright of heart, gladness. [12] Be glad, O righteous, in HASHEM, and give grateful praise at the mention of His Holy [Name].

כב־כג נָקִי יַרְשִׁיעוּ: וַיְהִי יְהוָה לִי לְמִשְׂגָּב וֵאלֹהַי לְצוּר מַחְסִי: וַיָּשֶׁב עֲלֵיהֶם ׀ אֶת־אוֹנָם וּבְרָעָתָם יַצְמִיתֵם יַצְמִיתֵם יְהוָה אֱלֹהֵינוּ:

א־ב לְכוּ נְרַנְּנָה לַיהוָה נָרִיעָה לְצוּר יִשְׁעֵנוּ: נְקַדְּמָה פָנָיו בְּתוֹדָה בִּזְמִרוֹת
ג־ד נָרִיעַ לוֹ: כִּי אֵל גָּדוֹל יְהוָה וּמֶלֶךְ גָּדוֹל עַל־כָּל־אֱלֹהִים: אֲשֶׁר בְּיָדוֹ
ה מֶחְקְרֵי־אָרֶץ וְתוֹעֲפֹת הָרִים לוֹ: אֲשֶׁר־לוֹ הַיָּם וְהוּא עָשָׂהוּ וְיַבֶּשֶׁת יָדָיו
ו־ז יָצָרוּ: בֹּאוּ נִשְׁתַּחֲוֶה וְנִכְרָעָה נִבְרְכָה לִפְנֵי־יְהוָה עֹשֵׂנוּ: כִּי הוּא אֱלֹהֵינוּ
ח וַאֲנַחְנוּ עַם מַרְעִיתוֹ וְצֹאן יָדוֹ הַיּוֹם אִם־בְּקֹלוֹ תִשְׁמָעוּ: אַל־תַּקְשׁוּ
ט לְבַבְכֶם כִּמְרִיבָה כְּיוֹם מַסָּה בַּמִּדְבָּר: אֲשֶׁר נִסּוּנִי אֲבוֹתֵיכֶם בְּחָנוּנִי גַּם־
י רָאוּ פָעֳלִי: אַרְבָּעִים שָׁנָה ׀ אָקוּט בְּדוֹר וָאֹמַר עַם תֹּעֵי לֵבָב הֵם וְהֵם
יא לֹא־יָדְעוּ דְרָכָי: אֲשֶׁר־נִשְׁבַּעְתִּי בְאַפִּי אִם־יְבֹאוּן אֶל־מְנוּחָתִי:

א־ב שִׁירוּ לַיהוָה שִׁיר חָדָשׁ שִׁירוּ לַיהוָה כָּל־הָאָרֶץ: שִׁירוּ לַיהוָה בָּרְכוּ
ג שְׁמוֹ בַּשְּׂרוּ מִיּוֹם־לְיוֹם יְשׁוּעָתוֹ: סַפְּרוּ בַגּוֹיִם כְּבוֹדוֹ בְּכָל־הָעַמִּים
ד־ה נִפְלְאוֹתָיו: כִּי גָדוֹל יְהוָה וּמְהֻלָּל מְאֹד נוֹרָא הוּא עַל־כָּל־אֱלֹהִים: כִּי ׀
ו כָּל־אֱלֹהֵי הָעַמִּים אֱלִילִים וַיהוָה שָׁמַיִם עָשָׂה: הוֹד־וְהָדָר לְפָנָיו עֹז
ז וְתִפְאֶרֶת בְּמִקְדָּשׁוֹ: הָבוּ לַיהוָה מִשְׁפְּחוֹת עַמִּים הָבוּ לַיהוָה כָּבוֹד וָעֹז:
ח־ט הָבוּ לַיהוָה כְּבוֹד שְׁמוֹ שְׂאוּ־מִנְחָה וּבֹאוּ לְחַצְרוֹתָיו: הִשְׁתַּחֲווּ לַיהוָה
י בְּהַדְרַת־קֹדֶשׁ חִילוּ מִפָּנָיו כָּל־הָאָרֶץ: אִמְרוּ בַגּוֹיִם ׀ יְהוָה מָלָךְ אַף־
יא תִּכּוֹן תֵּבֵל בַּל־תִּמּוֹט יָדִין עַמִּים בְּמֵישָׁרִים: יִשְׂמְחוּ הַשָּׁמַיִם וְתָגֵל
יב הָאָרֶץ יִרְעַם הַיָּם וּמְלֹאוֹ: יַעֲלֹז שָׂדַי וְכָל־אֲשֶׁר־בּוֹ אָז יְרַנְּנוּ כָּל־
יג עֲצֵי־יָעַר: לִפְנֵי יְהוָה ׀ כִּי בָא כִּי בָא לִשְׁפֹּט הָאָרֶץ יִשְׁפֹּט־תֵּבֵל בְּצֶדֶק
וְעַמִּים בֶּאֱמוּנָתוֹ:

א־ב יְהוָה מָלָךְ תָּגֵל הָאָרֶץ יִשְׂמְחוּ אִיִּים רַבִּים: עָנָן וַעֲרָפֶל סְבִיבָיו צֶדֶק
   _{כ לחדש}
ג־ד וּמִשְׁפָּט מְכוֹן כִּסְאוֹ: אֵשׁ לְפָנָיו תֵּלֵךְ וּתְלַהֵט סָבִיב צָרָיו: הֵאִירוּ בְרָקָיו
ה תֵּבֵל רָאֲתָה וַתָּחֵל הָאָרֶץ: הָרִים כַּדּוֹנַג נָמַסּוּ מִלִּפְנֵי יְהוָה מִלִּפְנֵי אֲדוֹן
ו־ז כָּל־הָאָרֶץ: הִגִּידוּ הַשָּׁמַיִם צִדְקוֹ וְרָאוּ כָל־הָעַמִּים כְּבוֹדוֹ: יֵבֹשׁוּ ׀ כָּל־
ח עֹבְדֵי פֶסֶל הַמִּתְהַלְלִים בָּאֱלִילִים הִשְׁתַּחֲווּ־לוֹ כָּל־אֱלֹהִים: שָׁמְעָה
ט וַתִּשְׂמַח ׀ צִיּוֹן וַתָּגֵלְנָה בְּנוֹת יְהוּדָה לְמַעַן מִשְׁפָּטֶיךָ יְהוָה: כִּי־אַתָּה
י יְהוָה עֶלְיוֹן עַל־כָּל־הָאָרֶץ מְאֹד נַעֲלֵיתָ עַל־כָּל־אֱלֹהִים: אֹהֲבֵי יְהוָה
יא שִׂנְאוּ רָע שֹׁמֵר נַפְשׁוֹת חֲסִידָיו מִיַּד רְשָׁעִים יַצִּילֵם: אוֹר זָרֻעַ לַצַּדִּיק
יב וּלְיִשְׁרֵי־לֵב שִׂמְחָה: שִׂמְחוּ צַדִּיקִים בַּיהוָה וְהוֹדוּ לְזֵכֶר קָדְשׁוֹ:

95:7. If we only heed God's call, He will end our travail and suffering even today.

95:8. *Meribah* means "strife"; *Massah* means "testing." See *Exodus* 17:1-7.

96:11. The components of nature exult in carrying out their assigned functions. The heavens give abundant rain, the earth gives generous crops, and so on *(Ibn Ezra)*

97:1. See 93:1.

97:2. The justice of God's ways is often masked by "cloud and darkness." In reality, however, everything He does is for a reason.

97:5. A metaphor for great and towering leaders.

98
A song of praise for the revelation of the final Redemption

A psalm! Sing to HASHEM a new song for He has done wonders; His own right hand and holy arm have helped Him. * ² HASHEM has made known His salvation; in the sight of the nations He revealed His righteousness. ³ He recalled His kindness and his faithfulness to the House of Israel; all ends of the earth have seen the salvation of our God. ⁴ Call out to HASHEM, all the earth; open your mouths in joyous songs and play music. ⁵ Play music to HASHEM on a harp, with harp and sound of chanted praise. ⁶ With trumpets and shofar sound, call out before the King, HASHEM. ⁷ The sea and its fullness will roar, the inhabited land and those who dwell therein; ⁸ rivers will clap hands, mountains will exult together ⁹ before HASHEM, for He will have arrived to judge the earth. He will judge the world with righteousness and peoples with fairness.

99
Once the nations acknowledge His sovereignty, they will follow the dictates of righteousness that Israel has safeguarded throughout its history.

¹ HASHEM has reigned: * Let peoples tremble; before Him Who is enthroned on Cherubim, let the earth quake. ² Before HASHEM Who is great in Zion and Who is exalted above all peoples. ³ Let them gratefully praise Your great and awesome Name; it is holy! ⁴ Mighty is the King, Who loves justice. You founded fairness. The justice and righteousness of Jacob, You have made. ⁵ Exalt HASHEM, our God, and bow at His footstool; He is holy! ⁶ Moses and Aaron were among His priests, * and Samuel among those who invoke His Name; they called upon HASHEM and He answered them. ⁷ In a pillar of cloud He spoke to them; they obeyed His testimonies and whatever decree He gave them. ⁸ HASHEM, our God, You answered them. A forgiving God were You because of them, yet an Avenger for their iniquities. ⁹ Exalt HASHEM, our God, and bow at His holy mountain; for holy is HASHEM, our God.

100
A psalm to accompany the thanksgiving-offering

¹ A psalm of thanksgiving, call out to HASHEM, all the earth. ² Serve HASHEM with gladness, * come before Him with joyous song. ³ Know that HASHEM, He is God; He made us and we are His, His people and the sheep of His pasture. ⁴ Enter His gates with thanksgiving, His courts with praise; give thanks to Him, bless His Name. ⁵ For HASHEM is good, His kindness endures forever, and from generation to generation is His faithfulness.

101
The traits of purity and truth enable an individual to utilize his abilities for their intended purpose.

¹ By David, a psalm. Of kindness and justice do I sing; to You, HASHEM, do I sing praise. ² I contemplate the way of perfect innocence, O when will You come to me? I walk constantly with innocence of heart within my house. ³ I do not place before my eyes any lawless thing; I despise doing wayward deeds, it does not cling to me. ⁴ A perverted heart shall remain removed from me; I shall not know evil. ⁵ He who slanders his neighbor in secret — him will I cut down [with rebuke]; one with haughty eyes and an expansive heart, him I cannot bear. ⁶ My eyes are upon the faithful of the land, that they may dwell with me; he who walks the way of perfect innocence, he shall serve me. ⁷ In the midst of my house shall not dwell a practitioner of deceit; one who tells lies shall not be established before my eyes. ⁸ Every morning I will cut down all the wicked of the land, to excise from the city of HASHEM all doers of evil.

102
A prayer for anyone beset by any misfortune

¹ A prayer of the afflicted man when he swoons, and pours forth his supplications before HASHEM: ² "HASHEM, hear my prayer, and let my cry reach You! ³ Hide not Your face from me on the day of my distress; incline Your ear to me, on the day that I call, answer me speedily. ⁴ For my days are consumed in smoke, and my bones are charred as a hearth. ⁵ Smitten

צח   א מִזְמוֹר שִׁירוּ לַיהוה ׀ שִׁיר חָדָשׁ כִּי־נִפְלָאוֹת עָשָׂה הוֹשִׁיעָה־לּוֹ יְמִינוֹ
ב-ג וּזְרוֹעַ קָדְשׁוֹ: הוֹדִיעַ יהוה יְשׁוּעָתוֹ לְעֵינֵי הַגּוֹיִם גִּלָּה צִדְקָתוֹ: זָכַר חַסְדּוֹ ׀
ד וֶאֱמוּנָתוֹ לְבֵית יִשְׂרָאֵל רָאוּ כָל־אַפְסֵי־אָרֶץ אֵת יְשׁוּעַת אֱלֹהֵינוּ: הָרִיעוּ
ה לַיהוה כָּל־הָאָרֶץ פִּצְחוּ וְרַנְּנוּ וְזַמֵּרוּ: זַמְּרוּ לַיהוה בְּכִנּוֹר בְּכִנּוֹר וְקוֹל
ו-ז זִמְרָה: בַּחֲצֹצְרוֹת וְקוֹל שׁוֹפָר הָרִיעוּ לִפְנֵי ׀ הַמֶּלֶךְ יהוה: יִרְעַם הַיָּם
ח-ט וּמְלֹאוֹ תֵּבֵל וְיֹשְׁבֵי בָהּ: נְהָרוֹת יִמְחֲאוּ־כָף יַחַד הָרִים יְרַנֵּנוּ: לִפְנֵי־יהוה
כִּי בָא לִשְׁפֹּט הָאָרֶץ יִשְׁפֹּט־תֵּבֵל בְּצֶדֶק וְעַמִּים בְּמֵישָׁרִים:

צט   א-ב יהוה מָלָךְ יִרְגְּזוּ עַמִּים יֹשֵׁב כְּרוּבִים תָּנוּט הָאָרֶץ: יהוה בְּצִיּוֹן גָּדוֹל וְרָם
ג-ד הוּא עַל־כָּל־הָעַמִּים: יוֹדוּ שִׁמְךָ גָּדוֹל וְנוֹרָא קָדוֹשׁ הוּא: וְעֹז מֶלֶךְ מִשְׁפָּט
ה אָהֵב אַתָּה כּוֹנַנְתָּ מֵישָׁרִים מִשְׁפָּט וּצְדָקָה בְּיַעֲקֹב ׀ אַתָּה עָשִׂיתָ: רוֹמְמוּ
ו יהוה אֱלֹהֵינוּ וְהִשְׁתַּחֲווּ לַהֲדֹם רַגְלָיו קָדוֹשׁ הוּא: מֹשֶׁה וְאַהֲרֹן ׀ בְּכֹהֲנָיו
ז וּשְׁמוּאֵל בְּקֹרְאֵי שְׁמוֹ קֹרִאים אֶל־יהוה וְהוּא יַעֲנֵם: בְּעַמּוּד עָנָן יְדַבֵּר
ח אֲלֵיהֶם שָׁמְרוּ עֵדֹתָיו וְחֹק נָתַן־לָמוֹ: יהוה אֱלֹהֵינוּ אַתָּה עֲנִיתָם אֵל נֹשֵׂא
ט הָיִיתָ לָהֶם וְנֹקֵם עַל־עֲלִילוֹתָם: רוֹמְמוּ יהוה אֱלֹהֵינוּ וְהִשְׁתַּחֲווּ לְהַר
קָדְשׁוֹ כִּי־קָדוֹשׁ יהוה אֱלֹהֵינוּ:

ק   א-ב מִזְמוֹר לְתוֹדָה הָרִיעוּ לַיהוה כָּל־הָאָרֶץ: עִבְדוּ אֶת־יהוה בְּשִׂמְחָה בֹּאוּ
ג לְפָנָיו בִּרְנָנָה: דְּעוּ כִּי־יהוה הוּא אֱלֹהִים הוּא־עָשָׂנוּ וְלֹא [°וְלוֹ ק] אֲנַחְנוּ
ד עַמּוֹ וְצֹאן מַרְעִיתוֹ: בֹּאוּ שְׁעָרָיו ׀ בְּתוֹדָה חֲצֵרֹתָיו בִּתְהִלָּה הוֹדוּ־לוֹ בָּרְכוּ
ה שְׁמוֹ: כִּי־טוֹב יהוה לְעוֹלָם חַסְדּוֹ וְעַד־דֹּר וָדֹר אֱמוּנָתוֹ:

קא   א-ב לְדָוִד מִזְמוֹר חֶסֶד־וּמִשְׁפָּט אָשִׁירָה לְךָ יהוה אֲזַמֵּרָה: אַשְׂכִּילָה ׀ בְּדֶרֶךְ
ג תָּמִים מָתַי תָּבוֹא אֵלָי אֶתְהַלֵּךְ בְּתָם־לְבָבִי בְּקֶרֶב בֵּיתִי: לֹא־אָשִׁית ׀
ד לְנֶגֶד עֵינַי דְּבַר־בְּלִיָּעַל עֲשֹׂה־סֵטִים שָׂנֵאתִי לֹא יִדְבַּק בִּי: לֵבָב עִקֵּשׁ
ה יָסוּר מִמֶּנִּי רָע לֹא אֵדָע: °מְלוֹשְׁנִי [°מְלָשְׁנִי ק] בַסֵּתֶר ׀ רֵעֵהוּ אוֹתוֹ
ו אַצְמִית גְּבַהּ־עֵינַיִם וּרְחַב לֵבָב אֹתוֹ לֹא אוּכָל: עֵינַי ׀ בְּנֶאֶמְנֵי־אֶרֶץ
ז לָשֶׁבֶת עִמָּדִי הֹלֵךְ בְּדֶרֶךְ תָּמִים הוּא יְשָׁרְתֵנִי: לֹא־יֵשֵׁב ׀ בְּקֶרֶב בֵּיתִי
ח עֹשֵׂה רְמִיָּה דֹּבֵר שְׁקָרִים לֹא־יִכּוֹן לְנֶגֶד עֵינָי: לַבְּקָרִים אַצְמִית כָּל־
רִשְׁעֵי־אָרֶץ לְהַכְרִית מֵעִיר־יהוה כָּל־פֹּעֲלֵי אָוֶן:

קב   א-ב תְּפִלָּה לְעָנִי כִי־יַעֲטֹף וְלִפְנֵי יהוה יִשְׁפֹּךְ שִׂיחוֹ: יהוה שִׁמְעָה תְפִלָּתִי
ג וְשַׁוְעָתִי אֵלֶיךָ תָבוֹא: אַל־תַּסְתֵּר פָּנֶיךָ ׀ מִמֶּנִּי בְּיוֹם צַר לִי הַטֵּה־אֵלַי אָזְנֶךָ
ד-ה בְּיוֹם אֶקְרָא מַהֵר עֲנֵנִי: כִּי־כָלוּ בְעָשָׁן יָמָי וְעַצְמוֹתַי כְּמוֹקֵד נִחָרוּ: הוּכָּה־

98:1. God requires no assistance. He acts through His "right hand," a term symbolic of power (*Radak*).

99:1. See 93:1.

99:6. During the inauguration of the Tabernacle, Moses served as *Kohen Gadol* (High Priest) for a seven-day period (see *Leviticus*, Chapter 8).

100:2. But in 2:11 we are told to "serve HASHEM with awe" — how can we reconcile gladness with awe? To feel fear, respect, and awe for God is essential to spiritual growth. Once a person realizes that his fear is the beginning of a process that leads to personal greatness and bliss, even the difficulties along the way can be accepted with gladness (*Ikkarim*).

I will prostrate myself toward Your Holy Sanctuary and I will acknowledge Your name, for your kindness and your truth, for you have exalted your promises even beyond you name. Psalms 138:2
Original Hebrew Translation

8

WORSHIP AND PRIDE DON'T MIX

We have to face the fact. We priests are cold to the Lord. We have not given him the reverence, the respect, the honor that he deserves. At least not the way they give him honor in Heaven before the throne. (Again read Revelations chapter 4, 5, and the rest of Revelations)

True worship will change our hearts. Man is prideful by nature. When he worships in a bowed position as well as a bowed heart (in truth and in spirit) man relinquishes that high position that he *imagines* he has. He not only confesses this privately, but publicly. Jesus said confess me before men and I will confess you before the Father. Are we embarrassed to bow down to the Lord before men? The Holy Spirit will soon show us our own hearts. The Lord himself bowed down before us when he washed Peter's feet. Can you imagine us being embarrassed before mere men to pay homage to the one who saved us from hell? Let's put our pride on the altar and burn it forever. Otherwise we will never be able to come near him. Pride is the root of Satan's failure. It is the root of man's failure.

Man does not easily detect pride, which is why Satan uses it as a weapon against man. Pride hinders man's relationship with God. That's why truly submitted worship, physically and spiritually, is the best antidote against pride. It spiritually teaches man his true relationship between himself and God and will quickly make man aware of God's never ending presence. This type of worship causes a true life changing experience in the life of God's children. Humbleness and humility before the Lord brings the true, perfect relationship between God and man.

Now is the time for the priests of the Lord to arise. The children of the living God, the ones who have not been born by the will of man, but he will of God. It's time for the church to worship God with the reverence he deserves. Not only daily in our prayer closets, but publicly in our services.

The presence of God, the weight of his glory shall fall as never before, like heavy rain when we see all our priests in one accord all bowed down before the Holy One of Israel. A Holy Hush will fall upon the entire sanctuary when we approach the Holy One according to the pattern of the heavenlies.

Unlike us, the Lord has no identity crisis. Many times in our Christian walk we always have to be encouraged by God himself. He encourages us, strengthens us, and gives victory always. The enemy attacks us and makes us feel discouraged and worthless. However, the Lord always manages to come at the right time to deliver us from such deceitful lies by Satan himself.

However, God never has that problem. He is always sure and confident of himself. He has no inferiority complexes. He knows exactly where he is, who he is, and where he is going. It is important for us to know who he is. It is important for us to know who we worship. Not only will this give us more confidence as to who we are in Christ because we have our being in God, the Father, the Son, and Holy Spirit, but it will also make us understand why we must reverence the Lord and give him the honor only he deserves.

Look to me and be saved all the ends of the Earth! I am God and there is no other. Isaiah 45:22

---

23. I have sworn by myself, the Word is gone out of my out in right eousness, and shall not return, that unto me every knee shall bow, every tongue shall swear. Isaiah 45:22-23

That in (at) the name of Jesus every knee should (must) bow, in Heaven and on Earth and under the Earth. Philippians 2:10

(The Lord plainly spoke to Moses) *I am the Lord your God, who has brought you out of the land of Egypt, out of the house of bondage.*

3. You shall have no other gods before or besides me.

5. You shall not bow down yourself to them or serve them; for I, the Lord your God, am a jealous God. The original Hebrew reads – You shall not prostrate yourself to them nor worship them, for I am Hashem, your God, a jealous God.

Exodus 0:2-3,5 (original Hebrew translation)

From the above verses, it is very easy to see who God is and what his heart is about.

Please note that the Jews were given *four distinct forms of divine worship* – prostration, slaughter, offerings upon the altar, and different liquids and wines upon the altar.

Offerings of animals and liquids are no longer needed because Jesus' flesh was the animal sacrifice and his blood was the liquid offering. The one divine form of worship, that has not been outdated but is a living, intricate part of worship, is of course prostration, bowing, and kneeling. We know this through the book of Revelations. *They still continue to prostrate themselves before God. This is the acceptable form of worship in Heaven.*

From the above scripture we also are warned by God not to prostrate ourselves and worship any other gods but him.

It is important to know our God's personal nature. When Moses asked to see his glory, the Lord said yes. All my goodness shall pass by you and I will proclaim my name **THE LORD** before you; for I will be gracious to whom I will be gracious and I will show mercy and loving-kindness to whom I will show mercy and loving-kindness.

See for yourself the nature of God. He has unfailing love, he is kind, merciful, slow to anger, and faithful. *This is his nature.* This is who we worship.

9

PEOPLE OF GOD WHO KNEW HOW TO WORSHIP ALWAYS CAPTURED GOD'S HEART

When Abram was ninety-nine years old, the Lord appeared to him and said, I am the Almighty God, walk and live habitually before me, and be perfect.

> *2. And I will make my covenant between you and me and will multiply you exceedingly.*
>
> *3. Then Abram on fell on his face and God said to him.* Genesis 17:1-3

You shall not prostrate yourself to them nor worship them; for I am Hashem, your God – a jealous God, who visits the sin of fathers upon children to the third and fourth generations, for my enemies

> *6. But who shows kindness for thousands (of generations) to those who love me and observe my commandments.*
>
> *21. An altar of Earth shall you make for me, and you shall slaughter near it your burnt offerings and your peace offerings, your flock and your herd; wherever I permit my name to be mentioned I shall come to you and bless you.* Exodus 20:5-6, 21 (Hebrew trans.)

Moses hastened to bow his face toward the ground, and prostrate himself.

14. For you shall not prostrate yourselves to an alien god for the very name of Hashem is "jealous one". He is a jealous God. Exodus 34:8,14 (Hebrew trans.)

Now when Daniel knew that the writing was signed, he went into his house, and his windows being open in his chamber toward Jerusalem, he got down upon his knees three times a day and prayed and gave thanks before his God as he has done previously. Daniel 6:10

It is not for you to do battle in this matter! Be erect, stand still, and see the salvation of Hashem for you O, Judah and Jerusalem. Do not fear and do not be broken! Tomorrow go out before them and Hashem will be with you.

18. Jehoshaphat bowed down with his face to the ground, and all of Judah and the inhabitants of Jerusalem fell down before Hashem to prostrate themselves to Hashem.

22. As soon as they began their exuberant song and praise, Hashem set up ambushers against the children of Ammon, Moab and Mount Seir who were attacking Judah and were struck down. Chronicles 20:17-18, 22 (Original Hebrew translation)

Please note when proper worship, divine worship, Heavenly worship, and acceptable legal worship is instituted, God supernaturally acts on behalf of his people – ALWAYS!

*And going a little further, **He threw himself upon the ground on his face** and prayed saying: My Father, if it is possible, let this cup pass away from me, nevertheless, not what I will (not what I desire) but as you will and desire.* Matthew 26:39

This for Jesus had to be one of the lowest moments in his life here on Earth. However, he knew how to approach God, not only in worship, but in his hour of need. *Flat on his face.* (Or in the Hebrew trans., prostrated himself before God)

And behold, a woman of the town who was an especially wicked sinner, when she learned that He was reclining at the table in the Pharisee's house, brought an alabaster flask of ointment (perfume).

38. And standing behind Him at his feet weeping, she began to wet His feet with (her) tears; And she wiped them with the hair of her head and kissed His feet (affectionately) and anointed them with the ointment (perfume).

44. Then turning toward the woman, He said to Simon, Do you see this woman? When I came into the house you gave me no water for My feet, but she has wet My feet with her tears and wiped them with her hair.

45. You gave me no kiss, but she from the moment I came in has not ceased (intermittently) to kiss My feet tenderly and caressingly.

46. You did not anoint My head with (cheap, ordinary) oil, but she has anointed My feet with (costly, rare) perfume.

47. Therefore I tell you, her sins, many (as they are) are forgiven her – because she has loved much. But he who is forgiven little, loves little.

48. And he said to her, Your sins are forgiven.

50. But Jesus said to the woman, Your faith has saved you; (enter) into peace (in freedom from all the distresses that are experienced as the result of sin). Luke 7:37-38, 44-48, 50

Please pay careful attention! Open your ears and see what the Spirit of God is telling you. Reread the above account of this particular woman. You will understand who this woman was and the condition of her heart. But more important, you will learn the condition of your own heart.

Let's first note this woman was not only a sinner, but a wicked sinner. She learned of the location of Jesus and came with expensive perfume. She knew without a doubt she had a need and she also knew who he was.

She immediately threw herself on her knees at his feet and cried. She took her hair and wiped his tear filled feet. She then kissed his feet and anointed them with expensive oil. This woman did not look around to see who was watching. She was not worried about looking foolish. She cared about only one thing, reaching the heart of the Son of God. She knew in her heart, no man could help her. Only the Son of God could. If she did not get his attention she was going to fade away into a dark lifeless eternity.

The so-called righteous ones were already pointing out how much of a sinner she was. They were already starting to criticize and make her out to be a foolish, good for nothing. Maybe they called her a show-off or an attention seeker. But, again, she did not care who said what. She kneeled at his feet and worshiped the King of Kings and Lord of Lords.

And, yes, Jesus responded! Thank God we have a savior who can see right through the pridefulness, the self righteous ones and pick up the lowly and desperate. You can see for yourself how he so responded to her love for him!

And now my dear friend, look to your own heart and see just how desperate you are. It does not matter if you are a pastor of a church of five thousand or the worship leader of that same church. It does not matter what you think you have accomplished for God.

If you can't come to church and bow, kneel, or prostrate yourself during worship, not sometimes, but each and every time you enter into the Holy of Holies in worship then you are cold to the Lord. You may be prideful, or ashamed of him. If you are not willing to approach the Holy One in the acceptable manor that the word of God has laid out for you, *you will never come close to him.* Standing or sitting is not acceptable. (Unless, of course, you have an knee injury.) Please, without his intimacy, without his presence, it's worse than anything imaginable. Please throw yourself at his feet and give yourself to him. Heart, soul, and body. While you still have your chance! It's not enough only to do it at home. You must confess him before men as your Lord. It's not enough to just say it. You must back it up by your heart and physical actions. It is than that he will confess you before the Father as a true worshipper of him.

And behold, a woman who was a Canaanite from that district came out with a (loud, troublesome, urgent) cry, begged. Have some mercy on me. O, Lord, Son of David! My daughter is miserably and distressingly and cruelly possessed by a demon.

23. But he did not answer her a word. And His disciples came and implored Him, saying send her away, for she is crying out after us.

24. He answered, I was sent only to the lost sheep of the house of Israel.

25. But she came and kneeling, worshiped Him and kept praying, Lord help me!

26. And he answered, it is not right (proper, becoming, or fair) to take the children's bread and throw it to the little dogs.

27. She said, Yes Lord, yet even the little pups (little whelps) eat the crumbs that fall from their (young) masters table.

28. Then Jesus answered her, O woman, great is your faith! Be it done for you as you wish. And her daughter was cured from that moment. Matthew 15:22-28

O beloved wake up and see what the Holy Spirit is teaching us. See and hear what the spirit is showing and saying to us. Jesus only came to the Jews while he walked the Earth. Salvation was for the Jews first.

But then comes a woman who was not a Jew. She calls him Lord. She begs for mercy. Jesus does not respond. At the same time his disciples opened their mouths and basically said, "get her out of here, she is not like us, she does not fit our mold."

My friend, you must get your eyes off of the dry dead formalism of the church. You must get your eyes off a dead legalistic form of worship and religion that Jesus does not identify with. The woman could have been discouraged not only because Jesus did not respond, but because man started to criticize her.

But then she employed what God accepts – pure priestly worship, which gives birth to *perseverance and endurance* with God. Then heaven started to respond.

She *dropped to her knees and worshiped.* She not only confessed him as God in front of everyone but backed her conviction up by honoring the Lord on her knees despite all that gossip and criticism in the background.

53

As Jesus saw this he responded by saying, I've only come for the Jews. You're not included. Instead of turning away, because of her acceptable and Godly worship a new boldness and wisdom was deposited in her from heaven. She was able to respond by agreeing with Jesus, however she also was proclaiming by her priestly worship that since he was Lord, he was more than able to meet the need of the hour, even if she could settle for the crumbs off of the table. The woman knew who he was. She acknowledges it by her worship. She had no doubt of his ability even if it were to be a leftover crumb. Her worship gave her a pure heart. A heart that would link her to heaven. A heart that surrendered everything that was flesh, and was resurrected to a heavenly faith that could not be denied. Her worship caused heaven to kiss earth and Jesus had to respond.

Will you respond to the Holy Spirit today? God is saying to you today, Come close. But you must approach me acceptably! Beloved, bow to the one who has eyes like fire. Whose feet are like bronze. Whose hair is white as snow. Who sits at the right hand of the Father. Who in heaven is worthy to open up the seventh seal. Who in heaven is known as the lamb of God, who takes away the sins of the world. Bow to our Father who created Heaven and Earth, who purchased you with the blood of his own Son, to make you a king and priest set apart for the worship of him.

The greatest apostle who ever lived, Paul, said –

I bow my knees to the Father of Our Lord Jesus Christ.
Ephesians 3:14

10

THE PRIESTHOOD

Each and every person who has ever been called and has accepted the Lord in their hearts has been given the position of a priest. Yet very few Christians have even the foggiest notion or the faintest idea of what this entails.

When we read Revelations 5:9-10 it says,
"And now they sing a new song saying, you are worthy to take the scroll and to break the seals that are on it, for you were slain (sacrificed) and with your blood you purchased men unto God from every tribe and language and people and nation. And you have made them a Kingdom (Royal Race) and Priests to our God, and they shall reign (as Kings) over the earth."

You shall be called the priests of the Lord: *people will speak of you as the MINISTERS OF OUR GOD.* Isaiah 61:6

*(Come) and like living stones, be yourselves built (into) a spiritual house, for a **holy, dedicated, consecrated priesthood** to offer up (those) spiritual sacrifices (that are) acceptable and pleasing to God through Jesus Christ.* 1 Peter 2:5

*But you are a chosen race a **royal priesthood**, a dedicated nation (God's) own purchased, special people, that you may set forth the wonderful deeds and display the virtues and perfections of him who called you out of darkness and into his marvelous light.* 1 Peter 2:9

Yes, you are not just somebody who has just said a prayer who goes to church, carries a Bible with them and makes sure that they say some prayers each day.

You are not just somebody who graduated Bible school, who is a pastor of a church of two thousand people. You are not just an evangelist who preaches to thousands of people each year. You are not just somebody who is a worship leader who leads singing on Sundays. You are not just a Christian writer who creates stories. You are not just somebody who is a Sunday school teacher, or a member of the choir, or the member of the board, or who is an usher, or someone who visits the sick in the hospitals, or visits those in jail, or who has a very successful business and gives thousands of dollars to the poor. This is only a small fraction of the definition of who you are in Christ.

You are a priest of the Living God. You are one who has been called to minister unto the most high. You have been called to be a worshipper in the Holy of Holies. *All these other jobs that you have been spending your life doing which I have named above should be work that has come out of your calling as a ministering priest to the Lord.*

For instance, if you are a pastor, you first calling is a priest, not a pastor. You are to fulfill your calling as a worshipping, ministering priest before you do your work as a pastor. You minister to God before you minister to man. Again, when you read above in Revelations, Christ purchased you with his blood to make you a priest. It does not say pastor. Again, your calling of a pastor comes out of your first calling of a priest. And so it goes with anything you do for the service of God. If not done in this order, your work done for the Lord is done out of the *flesh*. It does not matter how big your church is. Anything not done God's way is flesh. It has no eternal value. All things done for the kingdom of God must flow from the priesthood.

*For long ago (in Egypt) I broke your yoke and burst your bonds (**not that you might be free, but that you might serve me**)* Jeremiah 2:20

The highest call that any child of God has is to sit at the feet of the throne of God and to worship the Most High. God, the Father gave his most prized, precious possession to be slaughtered on the tree just so you and I could approach this throne to worship. This is why the veil was split at the Holy of Holies right after Jesus died on the cross. Yet most of the Body of Christ takes no advantage of this high privilege. Some Christians think church attendance along with fifteen minutes a day of prayer or reading of the word is sufficient. Others are running here, there, and everywhere doing this and that or building this and that for God.

I'm sorry to say this is not the perfect will for your life with the Lord. Again, your first calling and it does not matter who you are is to walk into your priesthood. To carry out your assignment of ministry to the Lord. This is the one single act that is your divine destiny. After ministering to the Lord, this is when God will cause you to expand the cords of your tent into other areas.

To understand your priesthood calling and to understand the intensity of its importance, we must go back to Exodus when God instituted the priesthood with Moses, Aaron, and his sons. There were very specific instructions to teach Aaron and his sons. After God instructed Moses to build the tabernacle for offerings, sacrifices, and worship, the priests were to be washed by water in front of the entire assembly of Israel. This signifies repentance and a cleansing of sins. As a priest today you must cleanse yourself thoroughly, not only once a day, but as often as you feel you need to do so. Sin has no place with a priest of God. Study the Word of God at least an hour a day. Why? Because it is through the word that God can convict you of things that are not right in your life. Not to condemn you but to strengthen you, and make you more into the image of His Son. The Word of God is also for the healing of your body. You must study the Word of God each and every day, as a priest this is your responsibility.

God commanded Moses what animals were to be used for the blood sacrifices. The animals were butchered right on the altar. The blood would be caught in a basin. The butchering of the animal sacrifices would cause an odor of blood that could be smelled throughout the entire town. The priests were instructed to take the blood and put it on their right thumb and right toe. The altar would also be soaked in blood. All this was done according to specifications. The shedding of this blood was for the forgiveness of sins. The priests were heaped in blood. This was their divine job.

Now, of course Jesus is the sacrificed lamb who was slaughtered on the altar. His blood is sprinkled on the mercy seat in the Holy of Holies. He is the perfect sacrifice. Each priest wore a specifically designed robe with a crown on their heads saying, "Holiness unto the Lord".

Now read this very carefully. You must understand the important position you have been given as a priest. *Only one priest a year could enter the tabernacle of the Holy of Holies. Only one.* It was Moses at first. The others had to stay on the outer courts. This one priest was given the job of the guilt offering in the Holy of Holies. This is how sin was forgiven for the entire country of Israel.

And now you have been given this high position as Moses. Yes, that's right. You and I have been given this high position of entering the Holy of Holies to minister to the Most High God. I will go one step further. We have been given an even higher position than Moses. Why? If you remember God would not allow even Moses to come too close to him. However, you and I have been given the invitation to come so close as to look into his eyes. We have been given the privilege of getting so close as to hear his heart beat and smell his fragrance. What a calling! What a position! Nothing in this world could be higher! Jesus has made the way for our priesthood. Jesus is the High Priest, the highest intercessor. He is called the priest after the order of Melchezedek, with no beginning or end. Now, since we have been crucified with Christ and it is no longer we who live, but Christ who lives inside us, we are now a high priest, a high intercessor. A priest after Melchezedek with no beginning or end. Do you understand the importance of your position?

We must, starting today, walk into this high calling. We must start now to understand the reality of God, that he is real. He sees all, hears all and wants to speak to us face to face.

As we mentioned before, repentance must be a natural order of things. You must strike the blood upon yourself and your family each and every day. If you should sin you must cleanse yourself immediately with the Blood of Christ and ask the Lord for the strength not to repeat the same sin.

This point cannot be overstated. The priesthood is absolutely the highest call a child of God has in his life. Nothing, I repeat, nothing in this world can have a higher calling than this.

The Lord is saying to you today, "You must strive to enter into this calling. You must with all of your mind, soul, and body devote yourself to this high calling of the priesthood. The world is dead to my priests. It has already been dissolved to them. There is no clinging to something that has already passed away. They have a new reality. That is my kingdom. My kingdom is for eternity. A priest's focus is on my kingdom. All he or she does is for the completion of the heavenly kingdom. Their ministering is for eternity and the consequences of their ministering is for eternity. Perishing souls can be snatched out of an eternity of fire by my heavenly priests. My priests, in addition to ministering to me, have to ability to demonstrate heaven on earth to give souls a glimpse of my kingdom here on earth. The Holy Spirit, which I give to empower my people, has the power to draw lost souls into my refuge. This is the call of a high priest. They are a heavenly being put on earth to demonstrate my reality. That is what means to be "born again". You have a new birth, which is from the heavenlies. "I, the Lord become your Father supernaturally by the Spirit that I implant in you. My kingdom becomes your kingdom. My ways become your ways. My nature becomes your nature."

Find your new life in the Holy of Holies, within the veil, which is the Holy of Holies. This is where I have my being and that is where you will have your being. The Holy Place is where you want to dwell. This is where the sacrifice is consumed. This is where the fire of my spirit burns brightly. This is where Holiness pours itself out to bring new resurrection power. The Holy of Holies is where transformation takes place. Nothing dark can be in the Holy of Holies. The light is too bright. Find your new life as a priest in the Holy of Holies.

11

WORSHIP

There have been many good faith preachers or pastors in the Body of Christ. You can find them on our Christian TV stations any day of the week, or in many of our churches preaching on Sundays.

The pastors have taught the Body of Christ well in the area of healing. When one is sick, we use scripture "by His stripes we are healed before we even see our healing manifested." This is called faith in our God as a healer.

When it comes to finances, we are taught to give before we have received. This is called faith in God as our supplier. We have been taught to speak to the mountain of problems before it is removed, and this is faith in our God as a deliverer.

However, when it comes to teaching the Body of Christ the reality of God in our midst the pastors and evangelists have missed the mark completely.

Our people have not been taught to acknowledge God's presence in worship services. Let me explain. If you were to go home to be with the Lord tomorrow and an angel escorted you into the throne room of God, what would be your reaction? The angel shows you the Father on His throne, Jesus on the other throne and all of heaven prostrating themselves before the throne. The angel leaves you in the throne room while he exits. You have a choice to make. You can either ask for a chair to sit, continue to stand and watch, or fall down on your face and worship. I would expect you to pick the last option and that is to fall on your face. This is the point. Why aren't you doing this now in worship? After all, you are in the Holy of Holies with the Lord in your midst. Do you believe this?

Let me use another example. You are in a Sunday worship service and the Lord manifests himself in smoke in the sanctuary. Will you continue to stand, will you sit, or will you fall to your knees or face? I would suspect you and the whole church would be on it's face. Again, this is the point. Does God have to blow smoke for you to get on your knees during worship? Do you see how ridiculous this is? We are showing absolutely no faith in the Lord being in our midst during worship services. We have mastered all the famous verses on getting things from God by confessing them before we get them. However, we have manifested absolutely no faith in our action when it comes to truly believing He is in our midst. Think about what you have just read. We walk by faith – not sight. The Lord has always said, "Let it be according to your faith." Let's prove our belief in him by worshipping as though he is there, because the truth is – **HE IS**!

To worship God is to manifest our statement that he is our creator and we are his creation and that everything we have in our life is dependent on him. Our true worship says to him that we understand we have been purchased with his son's blood. That our life is no longer our own but we are under his jurisdiction. We are here to serve him and not do our "own thing".

The second statement our worship makes is that we desire intimacy with him. *Nothing but the most intense love for him will ever satisfy him.* Our God's nature is loving kindness, unfailing live, mercy, compassion, slow to anger, and faithfulness. At the same time God tells us throughout the Bible to love him with all our heart, soul, and mind.

Hashem which is the Hebrew name for God is called the "jealous one". He is jealous for you. He loves you more than anything. He adores you and he will not share you with anyone.

One of our prayers should be to ask him to *enlarge our hearts* to love him *more than life itself. To love our neighbors* as ourselves. This fulfills his commandments. Only he can cause us to have a heart like this.

"The true Love of God is to obey his commandments". 1 John 5:3

We must learn to perfect our worship through the Holy Spirit. Worship holds the key to the throne room of God and true intense intimacy with him. Jesus said God is a Spirit. Those who worship him, must worship him in truth and in spirit. *For The Father Seeks Such Worshippers.*

Notice it says God seeks such worshippers. It does not say God seeks such pastors, evangelists, Sunday school teachers, etc. God is looking for special types of worshippers. When we pray, we seek God when we worship, *God seeks us.* Don't you want God to seek you? Of course you do! He will as long as you worship him in truth and in spirit, as long as you know the correct way to approach him. According to the scriptures, God always has "a way" for everything. He is not a "by chance" God. There is a unique divine order. Yes, God is a spirit. He is in a spiritual world that we must worship and enter into. We must be worshippers who know how to be heavenly worshippers and not earthly people who create a ritualistic, formalistic style that seems good, looks good but does not fulfill God's requirements.

Furthermore, when we worship in truth, we know Christ has enabled us to actually come into the Holy of Holies before the throne of God and meet with him. It's at this place God will meet with us and instruct us.

Everything Must Emanate From the True Heavenly Priesthood

Let everything we do, say, or think emanate from the priesthood and let our priesthood have its root source directly from the throne of God and Lamb of God in the heavenlies. This will be accomplished through our personal relationship with the Lord by sitting as his feet. Not only worshipping and praying, but staying in silence and waiting on him. This is the key. The waiting in silence. *Not Doing*. But just waiting. Just as the original priest waited at the tent of meeting for seven days until blessing the people. Again, if you are not willing, you can forget it. It is absolutely of no value. You must get rid of all of your pre-conceived ideas that have nothing to do with the Lord and his plans. We have beheld man and his ways for too long. We must behold the Holy One. We must behold the Lamb of God on the throne. We must behold only him alone.

This is attained by devoting ourselves as a priest to true worship, prayer, reading, and *Obeying* the word, fasting and holiness unto the Lord.

If you are reading this, God is speaking to you now. It is a decision you personally have to make. We have to count the cost. It's all of him or absolutely nothing. We can go on with this charade. As Paul the apostle said, "They have a form of Godliness but deny the power thereof." You may be saying, "That's not me" and I'm saying it is. What type of power is there in your faith that cannot even drive you to your knees in worship!

True priestly worship and dead religious formalism are on a collision course.

To be very basic and simple the meaning of "dead religious formalistic worship" is worship that is not orchestrated by God, it has no power, and conviction to drive a worshipper to his or her knees. It's a counterfeit, which seems good, looks good, but in reality it is make believe. It's cold, it's frigid, it's distant and has no relation to "Heaven's pattern of worship in the Holy of Holies."

The other choice we have is to choose God's way *and experience Him.*

When we do it God's way, we experience His true presence and glory individually and corporately. It's our choice. Yours and mine. God is saying to us, *Only those who bring me honor may come close* or another way of saying it is *those who come close to me must bring me honor.* Not the we think but the way the Lord wants honor, completely having its root source from the priesthood that originates from the heavenlies, which has been bathed in the blood of Jesus at the mercy seat of God.

The true glory of his presence will never drop in our personal lives or corporate church worship if we do not take this key of worship *And Use It* to unlock the door.

The Lord is saying to you today, "LOVE worship is what moves my heart, not form and ritualistic worship. Form and ritualistic worship is dead worship. It is blemished sacrifice that has no meaning to me. It does not come in spirit and in truth. It comes from a cold heart. LOVE worship comes from a heart of love for Me. Something I implant in prayer. I am the one who changes a stony heart to a heart of flesh. Ask and it shall be given to them who seek Me with all their hearts. The priests who shall come close to Me will be the ones who worship Me out of pure love and pure devotion for Me. These are the ones I seek."

12

WORSHIP, PRAYER, FASTING, READING AND OBEYING THE WORD

The working tools of a true priest are worship, prayer, fasting, reading of the word. A carpenter has tools to build a house. The better he masters those tools the better carpenter he is.

We must master our tools. This is our trade. A carpenter builds physical kingdoms. A priest builds spiritual kingdom. You must master every tool mentioned. Not some, but all of them. Without using all of these tools, the kingdom cannot be built. We are a priest forever, after the order of Melchezedek, with no beginning or end. This is our destiny, nothing more, nothing less. So, we must embrace our true trade. This is the sole function, our purpose in life.

Our Spirit Must Be Controlled By His Spirit

Our behavior controlled by his behavior. Our heart controlled by his heart. Our worship controlled by his worship. Our prayer controlled by his prayer. Our words controlled by his words. Our thoughts and meditation controlled by his. So on and so forth.

Hard? No, impossible! EXCEPT, EXCEPT, EXCEPT if you take your tools of prayer, worship, the word, fasting and begin to use them properly through God's instruction. Will you achieve it? Yes. God says in his own word that I will perfect that which concerns you. Period! But? No buts! NO CHEAP MAN MADE EXCUSES. It will be done on earth as it is in heaven.

How To Use Your Tools of the Priesthood

1. Worship – As a priest your purpose to your life, the reason for your existing is to worship God. The way you love your wife, husband, children, and people is a form of worship. The way you conduct yourself at work, the words you speak, the tithes, and offerings you give to the church are forms of worship.

However, I'm now speaking about the most intimate type of worship. The worship that should be taking place in the Holy of Holies at the throne of God where the mercy seat is sprinkled with the blood of Christ, who is the perfect sacrifice.

As a priest you have a supernatural right to enter this Most Holy place, boldly. You are to minister to the Lord daily in worship. The word says to enter his gates with a heart of thanksgiving and a mouthful of praise. After repenting and cleansing yourself in the blood of Jesus, you do exactly that. Thank God for what he has done for you. Don't take the Lord for granted for the things he does daily, perhaps the way we take our mates for granted for the things they do daily. Thank Him and praise Him. This is called being in the outer court. However, after thanking and praising him, we will move from the outer court to what we call the inner court or Holy of Holies. This is the "secret place". The Holy place. The throne room. This is where you will dwell. This is the place you will learn to worship God. Not man's way, but heaven's way. *You must ask the Lord, Lord take me higher into praise and worship, deeper into prayer intercession. Please orchestrate my worship from heaven. Let my words and song be orchestrated directly from the Throne of God and from the Lamb of God. Let my worship be nothing less than heavenly. Teach me what it is to worship in truth and spirit. Make me a Priestly Worshipper that you want to seek after.*

NO FLESH STANDS IN THE HOLY OF HOLIES

He will answer every word of this prayer. Why? Because that was the reason he purchased you with the blood of his son! For you to be that type of worshipper.

Read Revelations 4 and 5 over and over until the throne room is imprinted in your heart. Until the words that heaven uses to worship God become part of your heart and mouth. See for yourself how heaven bows down and prostrates itself before the throne of God. Read it until you become worship itself.

Advance to Revelations 7:9-17, then on to Rev. 11:15-19, and then on to Rev. 19:1-11. Finally Revelation 22. Again, *keep reading these verses each and every day until heaven becomes imprinted into your spirit.* Here in these verses the Holy Spirit will teach you how to worship God the way heaven worships. Here you will learn that the only way to approach God in the Holy of Holies is kneeling, bowing, or laying before him, but NEVER standing or sitting. No flesh stands or sits in the Holy of Holies. In your home or in corporate worship, it makes no difference. It is always the same!

In this Holy Place healing, deliverance, strengthening, wisdom, and impartation will take place. Worship should take place early in the morning and again in the evening. At least 30 minutes in the morning and at least 30 minutes in the evening should be a place to start with. God will teach you how to sing to him, how to make love to him. This is where intimacy is birthed. Never use the excuse that your voice is not good enough to sing to the Lord at home or in church. It is an insult to the Lord. The Lord gave you that voice. What you're saying is you're not appreciative of it. Instead, give thanks that you have a voice. God is not flesh. He is not interested in how sweet your voice is. He is much more interested in what kind of **"Sweet"-heart"** you are.

2. Prayer – This tool is used after worshipping. Prayer is your life line to God. It is your oxygen from heaven. Without it you will suffocate and die spiritually.

—·—

But we will continue to devote ourselves steadfastly to prayer and the ministry of the word. Acts 6:4

—·—

This says it all. They wanted God working through them. They did not just say it. They proved it in their actions.

If you take the dictionary and research the word "devote" it means, *to give up oneself to some person, purpose or service.* Giving up to a single purpose. *Shutting out everything else.*

Do you get the point?! Everything in their lives were given up except prayer.

Our attitude has to be the same. Yes, we have to go to work. Yes, we spend time with our families. However, it is then do we run back to our secret place that is reserved for God, and him alone.

Worship and prayer. Remember, this is your priority. Not a bunch of activities of doing. First hide yourself away with him. When he tells you to do, then do.

Throughout his life, with the disciples, Jesus spent entire nights praying to the Father. He encouraged the disciples continuously to pray without ceasing. To pray, to pray, to pray, to pray. As a priest of the Living God this is your trade, this is your vocation. Christ is the chief intercessor, the chief prayer warrior. You will step into your calling. You are an intercessor. You will be a prayer warrior. Why? Because this is what you have been called to do, period! This is not an option; it is your calling. You have been chosen for this. Each and every child of God has been chosen for this particular profession before anything else. Nothing in your life can come before worship and prayer. Nothing! Absolutely nothing! If it does, than anything you do outside of this worship and prayer *counts for absolutely nothing!* Because anything you do must be orchestrated from the throne room. Nothing can be orchestrated from the throne room unless there has been prayer to proceed the action.

Read Luke 6:12 Jesus went to the mountain and *prayed all* night.
1. Because he loved the Father.
2. He loved to be in communion with him.
3. Such was the love for his people that he had to in intercession.
4. He prayed when it was silent. No disturbances. It was a time of inaction.
5. While others found rest in sleep, *he refreshed himself with prayer.*

6.His place, none could intrude. None could observe.

7.Often his enemies were enraged. Prayer was his refuge and solace.

8.Prayer was the gate or entrance to his work, the beginning for new work.

Worship and prayer go hand and hand. Worship proceeds prayer. In Genesis 1:1, it says, the spirit hovered and then God spoke. First the spirit must hover or move, then God will speak. The spirit starts to move in worship. Most of the time proper worship is not performed and we attempt to speak. All we hear is flesh. Worship! Then the spirit will move. You must find a place where you can shut the door and be alone with God. Jesus says – Pray to your Father who is unseen. Jesus is telling us in advance that although our Father is unseen, he is there with open arms to welcome you. He is a spirit who you cannot see, but make no mistake, he is there. You must find a place for yourself where there are absolutely no disturbances. That's Jesus' first instruction. It's not an option. It's an explicit direction from the Lord. He wants absolutely no intrusion on your private meeting with him.

Ask Jesus to teach you how to pray the way he does. To get the same results as he does. To know the love of the Father the way he does.

So let's review. You selected a private place where there are no disturbances. You meet with him early in the morning before anyone arises. Perhaps maybe 4am, 5am, or 6am and also in the evening. Don't make it too late. Then you will be tired. Remember, the Lord comes first. Everything in your life comes afterwards. In the morning you come into the outer court by first cleansing yourself with the blood of Christ. Repent of all that has not been right between you, the Lord, and other people. Actions and thoughts are the same. Then you go into praise and thanksgiving. Worship is the next phase. Again, praise is giving honor to God for what he has done. Worship is giving honor to God for who he is.

The worship songs you sing can be the ones you have learned from church. Sometimes the Holy Spirit will give you a completely new song to sing. These come from your heart and are beautiful to the Lord. You may at times want to use some of your CD's that are your favorite to sing with. However, *only sometimes*. The reason is, if you only use the CD's to sing with, you will not have the opportunity for the Lord to allow the Holy Spirit to give you your own personal worship songs.

After you worship, ask the Lord for your different needs from anything to everything. Eventually the Lord will give you his desires for you and you will be more focused on what is truly important. Then you are to pray for all of the brothers and sisters in the Body of Christ. If you know their names, mention them. Pray for our governments and the president. Pray for the outpouring of the spirit upon God's people and make sure to pray for God to bring in true priestly worship into the Body of Christ. Ask him to use you to do it!

Let's talk about the time that should be spent each day in the presence of God. We always hear pastors say we should pray and worship but they never say how long. Somehow I get the impression they feel it's none of their business or that it's up to the individual. Not true! Prayer and worship are the pastors business because of the fact our lives depend on it. As a result, most of the Body of Christ has little or no prayer life. That is why we must address this "touchy" subject once and for all.

We always hear preaching on tithing and offerings. We are taught that we should give at least ten percent of our income for tithes, which is the Lord's. Plus offerings which are above that as our way of appreciation for what he has done for us. Again, that's bare minimum, because in truth everything belongs to the Lord.

If that be the case, then let's talk about tithes and offerings regarding our time to worship and pray. It would make all the sense in the world to realize God wants us at least "as much as he wants our money". Before I go on, God does not need our money. He wants us to give so that we may be blessed. Getting back to our prayer and worship, ten percent of twenty-four hours is two hours and forty minutes. This totals one hundred and sixty minutes. Throw in a twenty-minute offering per day and you get easily one hundred and eighty minutes a day in the presence of the Lord, uninterrupted.

Does it make sense to you? It should, it's not complicated. Church, God wants you. He is called the "jealous one". He created you for worship. *You are much more important to him than your dollar bills.* Don't neglect tithing and offerings out of your paycheck, but even more important, *don't neglect tithing and offerings out of your undisturbed time with him.*

Moses, Daniel, Ezekiel, Jeremiah, David, Jesus, Paul, Peter, James and John spent much more time than three hours per day in God's presence. This has to be our direction.

Please listen carefully. This is not for condemnation or to put guilt on you, and making you think you will never be able to do it. Here is the secret. Paul talked about being a boxer and training as an athlete. Bringing his body into submission. This is how you are going to do it. An athlete starts gradually. Not all at once. He starts running a quarter of a mile daily then increases gradually so as not to cause injury. He increases to a half mile, then to one mile, then two miles, and to three miles per day of running. The same is true with his weight lifting for strength. The boxer may start with fifty pound barbells, then one hundred pound, then to two hundred. All is done gradually as not to strain himself. In one-year time he has reached five miles per day of running, perhaps three hundred pounds of weight lifting. Now he is strengthened and prepared to meet his adversary.

You have to start somewhere and then increase from there. Add five minutes every third day to your intimate time with the Lord. Is it religious formalism? Not at all. It's called discipline. It's called getting yourself prepared to walk into your priestly calling to fulfill your destiny.

So, let's repeat it again. Start if you can with one half hour of worship in the morning. Add a half-hour of prayer with that giving you one hour of intimate time with the Lord in the morning. In the evening you should take the half an hour of worship with the Lord. Every third day you will add five minutes to the time spent with the Lord in the morning. *You will follow this program until you are spending at least three hours per day in the presence of the Lord.* Again, this is bare minimum. Your main prayer should be as Moses.

Lord, I want to behold your presence. I want all your goodness to pass by me, capture me, and then possess me. Enlarge my heart to love you more than life itself. Give me the grace to fall to the ground and die as a kernel of wheat and then be resurrected to new life. Give me the grace to allow you to live your life through me.

After your worship and prayer is done, wait in silence for the Lord, at least an additional half an hour. Always take a journal in with you. At the end of the 30 minutes just start writing. God is going to speak to you on a steady basis. You will learn that it could be either the Holy Spirit, the Father, or the Son. You will learn to recognize each of their voices. Yes, God has a voice. He speaks to those who are willing to listen and obey. Jesus said, "My sheep shall hear my voice." He will teach you everything you need to know about. Just start writing as thoughts come into your mind. You will soon realize what you are hearing, is his and not your own voice most of the time. Why? Because you will realize you don't have that kind of wisdom. The Lord will guide you about your marriage partner, your children, your prayer and worship life, the ministry, and instruction as on how to proceed. *This waiting on Him is more important than the doing.* Anything you will ever accomplish must come out of this patient waiting, God will mold you to his perfection in this time. After the priests would slaughter the animals when Moses, Aaron, and his sons performed the animal sacrifices they would wait at the tent of meeting for seven days, only after seven days, did they move out to bless the people.

Jesus fasted and prayed for forty days. It was a time of waiting on God. You and I have to wait also. Each and every day after your worship and prayer you must wait on the Lord. Some days you may hear nothing. However, on another day you may receive one word that will change your life. Do you want the real thing? Do you want to experience him in your individual life and powerfully in your corporate church services? Then wait on him that thirty minutes. Do nothing but wait on him. *This is more important than anything you do.* Deliverance, healing, strengthening, and impartation will take place during this waiting. He who waits upon the Lord shall renew his strength. He shall grow new wings as eagles. He shall run and not tire. He shall walk and not faint. Wait on the Lord in silence and patiently. If you do it, do it right!

3.The Bible – Your next tool is reading the word of God. This in addition to your worship and prayer life. Start with thirty minutes a day in the word. God speaks to you through his word. The word is health to your flesh. Get the Word of God rooted in your spirit. To know God's word is to know Him. Jesus said, "Man does not live by bread alone but by every word the proceeds from the mouth of God." The word of God will teach you how to live successfully and to die successfully. Death and life are in the power of the tongue. What comes out of your mouth can make the difference between living and dying. By getting God's word rooted in your heart, it will help assure you that your lips will utter God's word regardless of the situation.

4.Fasting – Probably one of the most powerful tools you possess as a priest and *hardly ever used by the Body of Christ*. When you pray, you seek to grasp onto God. When you fast, you let go of the world. They work hand in hand. Don't let anyone ever tell you that fasting is an option! Fasting is one of the most powerful weapons against Satan and his demonic forces that are trying to destroy you. This is not fairy tales. This is the truth! I've had conversations with pastors that have told me, "I will fast when God leads me to". That's as ridiculous as saying, "I will stop lusting after woman when I'm led by the spirit." That's crazy! The Word of God is the Word of God. It is sharper than a two-edged sword and will separate truth and lie as quick as you draw the sword.

Jesus was asked, "why don't your disciples fast often?" His reply was, "Because I'm here now. When I leave that is when they will fast often." Jesus also said in no uncertain terms that this kind of spirit only goes out by prayer and fasting.

Let me get right to the point. We want it all, the easy way. There is no easy way. The Lord never said the road was easy. He said he will be with us every step of the way to help us be successful as priests.

Fasting is a powerful tool to cause us to reach into the spiritual world.

You can compare fasting to being in a rocket to enter outer space. When you pray and worship, you are in a jet plane flying high. However when you include fasting it is actually transferring you from a jet plane to a rocket ship. *The rocket ship is able to pierce through the gravitational force of the earth and enter into outer space. This is how powerful fasting is.* I've heard all kinds of explanations of what fasting does. All I can tell you is if you want to reach God, if you want to see the Spirit move powerfully in your life, if you want to stop making believe and start reaching into the spiritual realm, start fasting regularly.

Moses wanted to reach God, so he fasted. All the prophets were hungry for God, so they fasted. Jesus, Paul, Peter, and James all fasted often and so reached into the heavenlies. If you are serious about God, fasting is no option. *Preachers should not be allowed on the pulpit if they are not men of fasting and prayer.* Without fasting all they are doing is reciting sermons on the pulpit. If they are fasting and praying, they are messengers of God. How often should you fast? Again, it's something you train for. Start with one meal. The next week, make it two meals. The third week three meals and the fourth week go over night to the next day. Drink water, eat no food. Try to work yourself up to the three consecutive days without eating. Ask the Lord for his grace to do it. He will be there for you.

Fasting is not a punishment. It is going to help you get a hold of God. You will see wondrous miracles taking place in your life.

I have given you an overview of what your tools are as a priest of the Living God. As a priest, your life is a life of prayer. In Malachi 2, God says his priests are messengers of God. Each of us are no less than this. The world is passing away. Souls are being lost to hell daily. We are the voice of God in the wilderness crying out,

"Prepare ye the way of the Lord. Repent for the kingdom of God is at hand. The ax is already laid at the root of the tree. Any tree that does not bear fruit will be cast into the fire".

That is the message to the world from heaven.

The message to God's people is,

"I want intimacy with you more than anything, but you must approach me heaven's way. The way I will be honored. Only those who honor me may come close to me."

You may say, "I have no time for all of this going on in my life. I'm too busy." I say to you, you probably are too busy. You have a free choice. A free will. It's completely your choice. That is why the Lord said, *"He who tries to save this life will lose the higher one"*, and *"He who loses this life will find the higher one"*, also, "He who would come after me must deny himself, pick up his cross, and follow me". Many walked away after Jesus spoke these eternal words. Many of us are still attached to this world, too much, not realizing that this world is not ours. Our kingdom is from above, not below.

I know in my own life, I've had to make decisions, important ones. Please, I'm sharing this with you, not so you will follow my way, but so you know I can identify with your struggles. *Jesus is the only one to follow.*

As a president of a marketing company, I've made decisions not to work most of Monday and Tuesday because those are the days I preach in Manhattan. I've made the decision to try to spend at least five hours per day in the presence of the Lord with worship, prayer, and reading of the word. To make time, I've had to get up as early as 3am to start so that I would have time to spend with the Lord. Sometimes I get tired and I get up at 5:30am, but more or less I keep to my schedule. When I come home at night I try to get at least one hour of worship in. Whatever it takes, your worship, prayer, and reading of the word *must come first!*

I fast mostly on Sunday's and Monday's until Tuesday morning after preaching. Sometimes I break my fasts prematurely because I break down and grab to eat whatever is around me. But you don't give up! You continue going and the next week you will succeed. This is real Christian living. We never fail. **The only time we fail is when we stop trying!** Never give up! Every mistake builds a learning block that you build on.

Love your wives, husbands, love your children, take them out, do things with them. But, again, never forget what you have been called to. It does not matter what title you have. Whether you are the president of a huge company or a pastor of a church of four thousand. Before all of this, your call is to the priesthood. You must fulfill your ministry of the priesthood. It is only out of this that your other callings have any validity. Otherwise it is only the work of the flesh.

13

GOD IS CALLING HIS PEOPLE TO THE TOP OF THE MOUNTAIN

1.*God is calling his people up to his high holy mountain to allow them to behold his presence and to let all his "goodness" pass by.* (Isaiah 2:1-3) This means not just praying but seeking the face of God until we meet him in a new experience. His word for his people who do this is, "I will not frustrate you". For the believer who understands this call, it means *cutting away all things in your life* that you possibly can and devote yourself to *worship* and *prayer* morning and evening & whenever you are able. This is the hour that God is calling his people to watch, pray, and fast that they can stand before the Son of Man.

Reasons:
a.The bride must prepare **herself**. Rev.19:7
b.The bride is not ready for Christ's return. We do not have extra oil for our lanterns.

Read and study Matthew 25:1-13. If we do not have enough oil (Holy Spirit) we will be part of the foolish virgins and suffer the consequences. The only way to get extra oil is to go up to the mountain of the Lord (not just to pray but seek his face (pursue God)) *Worship, prayer, fasting, & repentance- Meditate in his word.* We must repent *continuously* as we sin to keep ourselves undefiled before the Lord. (Ask for forgiveness from God and people who we sin against.)

This is the way we prepare ourselves as the bride. We must come into his presence and he will, "perfect that which concerns us."

This is not an option. God loves his people and wants us all in a "safe place." The Lord says, *"Rouse* yourself, *keep awake, strengthen* yourself, *invigorate* yourself, *stay alert, watch & pray."* "Do not be foolish." *It will mean disaster.*

Satan is launching an attack on the body of CHRIST more severe than ever before. He knows his time is short and his wrath will be poured out upon the ones he hates, "God's children". Satan will have the Body of CHRIST attacking each other with bitterness, slander, jealousy, and unforgiveness. The worst part will be that Christians will think that they are doing the work of the Lord by slandering other Christians. "A house divided against itself will fall."

a. The only place we will be able to defeat the enemy is from the "high places". The mountain top of God. We will not be able to defeat Satan and his army on his territory. The old way will not work. It never has, and especially now it will mean defeat for us if we attempt to do this. *We must go now* to the mountain of God and allow God to prepare us for war with the enemy.

b. As we *separate* ourselves unto God and start to ascend the mountain we will find ourselves being attacked by the enemy through *distraction, fear, and intimidation.* (Read the book of Nehemiah) The enemy will allow you to do many activities for God but the "one thing he will not tolerate is you seeking the face of the Lord". It is here where you will be *healed* by him in *all areas* through *pure worship and truly empowered* to advance against the kingdom of darkness. Not only will the spirit fill us but also as Jesus was, *we all must walk in the power of the spirit.*

Encouragement

We will all have to predetermine to ascend the mountain. No matter what happens or the cost. The wind and rain will beat upon us. This represents the attacks of the enemy (distractions, persecutions). Nevertheless, if we set our faces *like a flint* to ascend the mountain of the Lord, with the Lord's help we will make it to the top. There will be times when we might fall climbing. It may be a day, maybe a week. It does not matter, *keep climbing and don't stop. Don't stop* no matter what. *Don't look back!* Don't look back! Not yet! Not until we reach the top and see Him. His glory. His goodness. His love, compassion, and mercy. Not an echo of him, not a trace of where he was yesterday or where he will be tomorrow, *but where he is RIGHT NOW!*

Be encouraged our brothers & sisters to ascend this mountain. This is the climax of our faith. This is where heaven will kiss earth. It will be all worth the cost, which in comparison will be very little. In His presence, on the top of His holy hill, we will experience "the Father's love'. It will be our daily bread. His love will heal us.

Revive us, strengthen us and equip us for victory because his love never fails. It is the greatest of all the gifts. The most powerful of all gifts. That's why the apostle Paul said, "Aim for it, strive for it." Make it your quest. The Gift of Love. Truly experiencing the Father's love in the fullness of his presence will *take the veils off our eyes* that we may see clearly. This is what Jesus spoke about in Revelations 3:18 when he said, "I counsel you to purchase from me gold refined and tested by fire, that you may be truly wealthy and white clothes to clothe you and keep the shame of your nudity from being seen and *salve to put on your eyes that you may see.*" The enemy has led the body of Christ to a false finish line. Attend your church service, do your ministry that God has given you, read your Bible and pray a little. All is well. Jesus is coming soon and all is well. It's not well! We are blind, deaf, and dumb. We are not seeing through the eyes of God. We know Jesus as the Lamb of God but do not know him as the LION OF JUDAH – the

RIGHTEOUS JUDGE. We must know both. Again, examine Matthew 25:1-46. He is talking to the Body of Christ. Not unbelievers. We must labor to enter into his rest.

The trumpet is blowing, sounding the alarm to come up to his holy mountain. Can you hear it, can you hear it? *Please wake up before it is too late.* Seek his face to behold his presence as Moses saw all the miracles that nobody has seen he still knew they were just manifestations. That is why his last request was "Lord, show me your glory!" The most exciting thing is, because Jesus had not yet come and the veil was not torn. God still had to say to him, "Don't come to close." But we have been granted the privilege because of the veil being torn and access into the holy of holiness is ours. We can come into our Fathers lap and look into his eyes and be transformed immediately. Yet we have not taken the advantage of the great call. The time is now, not tomorrow. We must all make a predetermined decision to climb his holy mountain. Our eyes will open in his presence to see as never before. The Father's love as it burns off the veil from over our eyes. It will enable us to see with such clarity as never before. The strategies of the enemy, the qualities we have lacked, the *false motives* for doing good, the misuse of the talents that God has given us and the *pride* that we have managed to acquire as Christians. This opening of our eyes will not be for condemnation but for our correction for the Lord corrects those who he dearly loves.

From the top of this mountain the Lord will truly teach us the meaning of his words. He who will try to save his life will *lose it* and he who loses his life will find the *higher one.* He will teach us the meaning of, "We have been crucified with Christ". It is no longer we who live, but Christ who lives inside us. He will teach us that we can fall from any level. That any man who thinks he stands beware lest he fall. He will make us to understand that no matter how big the ministries we have, once pride enters the picture, once we think it's *our ministry*, once our motives become perverted that we want people to be drawn to us along with Christ, the works become *useless* and are no value. Our brothers and sisters in Christ who have been given much authority and power with large ministries please take heed. We must examine ourselves and it can only be seen in his presence how pure our motives are.

Pride is the hardest of all the arrows that the enemy shoots at us to see. It blinds us, it can destroy us. It's so hard to defeat because it hits us from the back.

Drop what you're doing and come up to the mountain to seek the face of the Lord.

Take up your cross daily, putting all you have and all you are before him at his feet. Wash his feet with your hair.

Do not look at you. Become blind to you. Return to the cross. Preach. Christ *crucified* and *risen*. The *power* is at the *cross*. The *power* is in the *blood*. Stop criticizing other denominations, throw your religion and denomination out the window and preach Christ and the cross.

Love the Savior – seek his glory *Alone*. Love the Savior by obeying his commandments. 1 John 5:3

Let's live our lives for his glory. Live what we preach.

No matter what you do, walk in love.

Meditate on the word. Read 1 Corinthians 13 and do what it says. Love does not seek its own.

We will be changed and understand when we behold His glory with an unveiled face. Beholding our Father's love will remove the veils – GO TO THE MOUNTAIN!

We will overcome this world by his love – GO TO THE MOUNTAIN!

Stop judging by appearances but by his wisdom only. Wisdom is to see with His eyes. GO UP TO THE MOUNTAIN!

Compassion will remove many veils from your soul. GO TO THE MOUNTAIN!

Remember the homeless, orphans, and widows. When you love them you will always receive the

Lord's help. You will be given more of the helper (Holy Spirit) by the measure of your love. GO UP TO THE MOUNTAIN!

Love those who the Lord loves and you will receive more of the anointing.

Do not gossip or slander, but instead forgive and love. Encourage, correct, warn, but always in love.

We are not asked to sacrifice. Jesus already did that. We are asked to obey. In obeying we may have to sacrifice. Go to the Mountain.

If you react to guilt, you will do things in compensation for your guilt. This is an affront to the cross.

The cross alone removes guilt because Jesus went to the cross to remove the guilt. Whatever is done out of guilt is not done for the Lamb. Go to the Mountain.

Love is our greatest weapon. *Love* never fails. Love is the weapon that destroys the works of the Devil. Look what Jesus did on the cross out of love. *Love* is what will bring the kingdom of the Lord. *Love* is the banner over the Lord's Army. Use your banner of love to defeat the enemy.

Awake O sleeper – NOW! There is no time left. These are the end of the latter days. Come let us go up to the Mountain of the Lord to the House the God of Jacob. Let us learn his ways and walk in the light as he is in the light.

Can you understand what you have just read? Those of you who have ears, listen to what the Spirit is saying. Those of you who have eyes, see what the Spirit is saying.

You must drop the things in your life that really have no eternal value like watching TV, reading senseless books, and many other activities that may not necessarily be sin but are taking time away from being in his presence, worshipping, praising, and praying.

Many may read this warning and think it overly dramatic but I pray that we all take heed to the voice of the Lord as one crying in the wilderness. We do not have enough oil yet. The Lord is faithful and loves us enough to prepare us by giving us enough time to prepare for the journey up to his holy mountain. Come now my brothers and sisters. Come let's hold hands and *encourage each other* to go up to the mountain. Come; drop what you're doing! There is no time to waste! Don't procrastinate!

Don't be left behind! Come let us go!

End Note I:

The meaning of going up to the Mountain specifically means to seek God, pursue God. Don't stop until we have a new experience, a new encounter. Make it a priority of our lives. Worship, praise, and of course, prayer and fasting.

End Note II:

Prayer and fasting. You can't have one without the other. The church has been robbed of its glorious

Power. Why? Because fasting is our most powerful tool and Satan has robbed the body of Christ.

Jesus, plus all the apostles, and all the Old Testament prophets knew the power of prayer and fasting.

Yet today fasting is rarely spoken of. No fasting – No power. No fasting – No power. Every scripture confirms it.

14

THE BLUEPRINT FOR TRUE THRONE ROOM WORSHIP

(As to Allow the Presence and The Glory of God to Fall)

By now you have read most of this message. Whenever there is prophetic revelation you must weigh what you read or hear. Number one: *Is the message about giving glory to God or man?* Number two: *Does it line up with the Word of God?* If you are a child of God you have been called to sit at the feet of Jesus. You must read this chapter line by line. If there is anything you don't agree with because you think it does not line up with the Word of God underline it with a yellow marker and call me. I'm always available for you. If it's truth, you must act immediately and make necessary changes.

Yes, there is a blueprint for everything we do for God. God is not haphazard. He is not a "by accident" God. Before he moves, he tells us.

God is about to make a right turn.

Let me repeat myself. *God is about to make a right turn.* What am I saying? Just this. As a whole body we have been praying to God to have his presence or his glory fall on us. The Lord will not frustrate his own children anymore than we would frustrate our own if they wanted us draw closer to them. God is not going to make us jump through hoops to touch him.

He is inviting us to come close. To experience him in a way we have never experienced him before. Again, he must be approached as heaven approaches him. Those who come close to him must honor him. Here is the blueprint that you are to follow.

The present state of your worship service must be uprooted and replanted.

Pastors, you are to walk in your priesthood and fulfill your calling in that area as outlined in the previous chapters. You must meet with your worship leaders and tell them the direction you are going. That is to seek the presence of God in its fullness. To get away from your "ordinary services" that has its usual beginning, middle, and end. *Your goal is to have God take control of the service.* Your worship leader and elders must be instructed about their high call as a priest first. Most truly don't have the revelation of what it is.

You will know it immediately by asking them about their individual worship and prayer life. Yes, as a pastor it is your business. Proverbs says to, "Know the state of your flocks." Know where you are and know where you want to go.

You must get yourself and your staff into a life of worship, prayer, reading of the word, and fasting immediately. If the heads are not devoting themselves to it, how do you expect the flock to ever enter into it?

You must bring your flock into repentance, a constant state of repentance. You must teach your flock the priesthood and how they must enter into it. Again, as outlined in the previous chapters, you must make them very clear on the fact that each and every day of the week, morning and evening, they must devote themselves to the Lord.

You must make them aware they must prepare themselves before each service. Not only them, but you too. Worship, prayer, and fasting are a definite agenda. The church should not be eating breakfast before they come to service. The preacher should have spent at least Saturday locked up in his room with God without eating. Sunday morning before service the same thing. The preacher on the pulpit must be sensitive to the Spirit of God, not sensitive to the spirit in his belly that cries out night and day, "feed my flesh!" You say you hear even though you eat. The spirit says, "You think you hear but you're fooling yourself!"

If Jesus had to fast to hear the voice of the Father, as well as Paul, we certainly are no better than they.

There is no quick way. Only the true way, which is the thruway to heaven.

Your worship leader must be a man of prayer and fasting. Again, he too must be sensitive to the spirit. *He must pray to God to orchestrate all worship to match the pattern of worship to heavenly worship.* The words of the worship song must match up with the words sung in heaven. Again, have the worship leader study Revelations 4 and 5.

The worship leader cannot preplan how many songs are to be sung. Let the Holy Spirit determine this. Yes, the Holy Spirit wants the Father to be glorified as well as the Son. Sometimes there will be silence between worship songs. That's fine. Listen and wait on him. The worship leader must lead. He must take the congregation from praise, which is on the outer court into the inner court, which is the Holy of Holies. Until the congregation gets sensitive to know when this transition takes place, he must announce to the congregation that we are about to enter into the most intense place, the Throne Room of God. By the mercy seat, which is sprinkled by the blood of Jesus. He must announce and remind the congregation that those who wish to enter into this place, those who want to come near Him who sits on the throne must come up to the front, at the altar.

The congregation should be able to fill all the space available, even on the stage itself, but everyone must be either on their knees, bowed down, or lying down (prostrated before God). Ushers must prepare in advance to cover those who need to be covered with blankets so that decency and order is maintained.

Of course, all this should have been preached to the congregation a week or two in advance by the pastor to make sure that everyone is aware of why we are doing what we are doing. This will not be a surprise but will only come out of what the Spirit is already taught the congregation.

I will be available to preach this message to your congregation if you desire. Worship at this point must not be rushed. God is not in a rush, only we are to get to the next part of the service. *Get rid of that attitude.* You can't fool God. If you want him than mean it. Don't honor him with your lips and have hearts that are far from him. Wait on him. Wait in silence. Wait. Worship stirs the Spirit. Only after the Spirit starts moving will you then start to speak. Done in its proper order, your messages will change. Your words will be like a hammer breaking rock. God will move in ways so different. You will have to be prayed up to be sensitive to the leading of the Spirit. Don't be afraid to wait for him in silence. This is when the deepest work is done by the Holy Spirit to the body of Christ – in that place of waiting.

Let me clarify something. From the beginning of the service to the time people come up to worship, when the preaching is about to begin the pastor will announce to the congregation they may return to their seats. After the message has been given, worship will probably start again. This time it will probably be the pastor calling the people to enter into the Holy of Holies. People will come to the front wherever there is space, kneeling, bowing, and prostrating. These are the three acceptable forms of worship in the Holy of Holies and will be expressed at this time.

There may be times when the spirit signals the pastor to speak without sending anyone back to their seat. This is entirely up to the pastor working in conjunction with the worship leader and ushers. There may be times when God wants to send healing through the body. The Lord can do it automatically or may want to invoke prayer teams to lay hands on people. You as a pastor must be prepared and sensitive. Nothing is ever the same when God is in control!

Does this sound strange for you to handle? Perhaps. Many disciples walked away when Jesus said they must drink his blood and eat his body. Many turned and left. You have a choice also. You can continue to walk in the path you are going with dead ritualistic worship that has nothing to do with heaven. It gives no honor to God and therefore those who give no honor to God shall not come close.

However, God loves you so much that he is reaching out his hand to you and saying "Rise and come forth. Come close and give me honor before the congregation and before the world."

Those who honor me, there I will make my true resting-place. It is there that I will meet with them and instruct them. My presence they shall experience as never before.

I will leave you with these last scriptures that are translated from the original Hebrew. Please just sit back and let the Holy Spirit minister to you now.

(This comes directly right from the mouth of Almighty God. Whose Hebrew name is Hashem, it means the merciful one). He is called the "jealous one".

For just as the new heavens and the new earth that I will make will endure before me-the word of Hashem-so will your offspring and your name endure. Verse 23: **It shall be that at every new moon and on every Sabbath all mankind will come to prostrate themselves before me, says Hashem.** Isaiah 66:22-23

Please, Please, Please! *Open* your eyes and *see* what God is saying above in the scriptures. In the New Kingdoms he will create, he is showing us the proper way to honor him, the proper way to approach him. It is to *prostrate* yourself, *bow down* or kneel down before him. There is no other way. This is not an old-fashioned way to worship. It is an *eternal way.* A way that would never be outdated.

Again, look at Isaiah 66:2.

But this is the man to whom I will look and have regard; he who is humbled and of a broken or wounded spirit and who trembles at my word and reveres my commandments. Isaiah 66:2

We have a choice to make! It is either to resist the Holy Spirit, and continue in our dead ritualistic form of religious worship and only seeing the Lord from afar, or we can respond with all that is in us to accept this intimate invitation of drawing so close to Him as to hear his heartbeat and smell his fragrance. I urge you, *bow your heart, drop to your knees, fall down upon the ground* before Him and worship the One and Only True God!!! Wherever you are, at home or in the church, give honor to Him, that he alone deserves.

Glory and majesty are before him, might and splendor in his sanctuary. Verse 7: *Render unto Hashem O families of the peoples, render unto Hashem honor and might.* Verse 8: *Render unto Hashem honor worthy of his name; take an offering and come to his courtyards* **Prostrate yourselves before Hashem in his intensely Holy place;** *tremble before Him; everyone on earth* Verse 10: *Declare among the nations, "Hashem has reigned!"* Psalms 96:6-10 (Original Hebrew Translation)

Exalt Hashem, our God and Bow at his footstool; He is Holy! Verse 9: *Exalt, Hashem, our God, and Bow at his holy mountain; for holy is Hashem, our God.*
Psalms 99:5,9 (Original Hebrew Translation)

Even if you are the only one in your church on the floor, let God use you to bring others to the feet of our Holy God!

He who has ears, hear what the Spirit has said.

He who has ears to hear, let him be listening
and let him consider and understand by hearing!

About The Author

The author is the Holy Spirit, which has no beginning and no end. He is from the eternities to the eternities. When Christ ascended to the Father, He was sent to every true believer as the teacher, comforter, counselor, and strengthener.

My name is Jack Toback. The only credit I will take for this book is that I am the one who wrote down what the Spirit was saying. I am not smart enough nor do I have the wisdom myself to write down the astonishing truths, which have been hidden from the church regarding worship. They have been revealed to you personally in this book.

My birthday is April 17, 1945. I was born a Jew. I rejected Christ as the Son of God until 1981. He came to me personally while I was in a Zen Buddha Temple. Twenty-one days later he came a second time and changed my heart in an instant. I was born again from above! I'm married with 5 children. My occupation is President of a marketing company. I've been a New York City street evangelist over eighteen years. I was preaching the day the towers fell in New York City.

A. I preach Christ crucified and risen. For the Jew first, and then for the Gentile.
B. I believe I can do nothing without Christ.
C. I believe every believer is called as a priest unto the Most High God.

D. I believe we manifest our faith by our love for God, the Son, the Holy Spirit, our wives, children, the body of Christ, and the world.

E. I believe that our single most important reason for being is to sit at the feet of the Father, the Son, and the Holy Spirit and worship them.

F. I believe in fasting and prayer.

G. I believe that at "the name of Jesus Christ every knee shall bow and every tongue shall confess that Jesus Christ is Lord to the Glory of the Father."

H. I believe that you personally and your church corporately will now experience the greatest manifestation of God's presence you have ever known as long as you embrace the "key" which is given to you now by the Holy Spirit in this book.

I. *Render unto Hashem the Honor is due his name. Honor Hashem the Lord, bow down before him in the Beauty of Holiness.* Psalms 29:2